P9-CQO-060

"College is still one of the greatest avenues to personal opportunity in the world. But the stakes now are higher, and the financial investment demands that we make good choices about where and how to pursue education. There is no better guide than the thoughtful and insightful Michael Horn to help us understand what matters in college, what we can expect from a degree, and how to make the most of the college experience. If you are looking for one book to guide your choice, start here!"

Mary B. Marcy, President, Dominican University of California

"In *Choosing College* Michael B. Horn and Bob Moesta dive into the complexities of making learning decisions and emerge with clear, compassionate guidelines for both learners and educators."

Adele Faber, co-author of How To Talk So Kids Can Learn

Does the world need yet another college guide book? It most certainly needs this fresh and insightful book from Michael Horn, who eschews the usual catalog of college profiles and instead focuses on the prospective student and the jobs they need college to do for them, Based on research, thousands of student profiles, and informed by a deep understanding of higher education, *Choosing College* should be read together by students and their families and used as a way to frame the often fraught conversation about choosing the right college. Choosing the right college remains an often befuddling and irrational process. This book changes all that, not because it provides better answers. It provides better questions, and that's what has long been needed. If you are considering college, this should be the first book you read. It may be the only one you'll need.

Paul LeBlanc, president of Southern New Hampshire University

This is a friendly, pragmatic, accessible guide demystifying what is an often intimidating and stressful decision attended by an intimidating and stressful process. The authors focus on self-knowledge and the all-important personal "why"—why college, why now, why a particular type of institution, etc., rather than the elitist, extrinsic agenda-driven approach of too many college guides. I wish we'd had this book when our children were making their higher education decisions; I wish I'd had it when I was making mine.

Whitney Johnson, Thinkers50 Management Thinkers and best-selling author of Build an A Team *and* Disrupt Yourself

In offering 21st century advice in *Choosing College* to students and parents about what to seek in a college experience, Michael Horn and Bob Moesta also lead counselors, teachers, and higher education leaders to examine what they are offering today's applicants. Introducing "The Jobs to Be Done" concept is a practical guide for sparking reflection, relevance, and renewal across the teaching and learning spectrum. I found how

Horn and Moesta provide personal human stories on top of extensive data to be extremely effective driving home key points. This book provides an engaging approach to students and parents making critical decisions about college; even better, it pushes higher education leaders to make decisions that will sharpen their institution's relevance to learners with different needs. And for policymakers confronting tough decisions about higher education, *Choosing College* is a good starting point for matching how well a state's institutions are meeting today's student and workforce needs.

Bob Wise, former West Virginia governor
and congressman

3 options: Horn and Moesta's "Jobs to Be Done" model can lower the stress and confusion caused by the multitude of higher education options and career choices. Not only does this book teach students and their parents how to explore education and career options, but it also demonstrates how they can have a positive dialog during the process. Colleges and universities can also gain insights from exploring this framework as a new approach to understanding how learning experiences and student life circumstances can better connect.

The strength of American higher education is that it provides so many pathways, but this rich tapestry of options can appear to students as confusing and stressful. Through the framework presented by Horn and Moesta, learners can start to understand why they are seeking more education and what a college or university experience might accomplish in relation to their life goals. Colleges and universities can also gain insights from exploring this framework as a new approach to understanding how learning experiences and student life circumstances can better connect.

Jerry Weber, president of Bellevue Community College

Too many books focus on how to get into college without starting with the more fundamental question: Why are you going and how will you make it count? Horn and Moesta have developed a powerful framework to help students, and the adults who support them, put purpose and agency at the heart of the college decision process. And the world will be better for it!

Abby Falik, founder and CEO of Global Citizen Year

Choosing College removes the mystery around educational choices and provides a framework to help people deeply understand why they are considering more education . . . . this book gives them the knowledge and tools to make the right life decisions. This is a critically important and timely work that should be read by all who want to advance their lives through learning.

Don Kilburn, CEO University of MA Online and former president of Pearson North America

Horn and Moesta shed novel light on what is really at work when students choose college. By helping us all focus on what we really seek from college and therefore what really matters to us, they open up rich new terrain for thinking better about one of the most important, and often expensive, choices we make. As a parent, this book helped me rise above brand chasing toward smart matching. As a leader in higher education, this feels like a needed wake-up call at a crucial moment in history to setting mission and focusing priorities for institutions to move beyond trying to be all things to all people.

Chris Gabrieli, chairman, Massachusetts Boar of Higher Education and lecturer, Harvard Graduate School of Education

Choosing to attend or return to college is a critical life decision. Students "hire" a college to do many things. But many prospective students don't fully recognize the criteria on which to make their choice. Sometimes educational "jobs-to-be-done" are well understood and sometimes they are more tacit. Michael Horn and Bob Moesta have captured and articulated the jobs students hire a college to do in a compelling and intuitive way. Better understanding these jobs can more effectively inform student choice. It can also better inform how colleges and universities can serve students and the jobs they are hired to do through their education. This book is as helpful to the prospective student as it is to the university administrator. *Choosing College* provides a significant contribution to the work of higher education and our collective efforts to better serve students.

Clark Gilbert, president of Brigham Young University Pathway Worldwide and former president of Brigham Young University-Idaho

Michael Horn and Bob Moesta deliver insight after insight about why students choose college ... and how to serve them better. A roadmap for leaders in the new world of higher education.

Alex Hernandez, dean, University of Virginia School of Continuing and Professional Studies

For almost every individual, the question of college - whether to go, where to go, what major - is one of those life-changing decisions? And while the data continue to support the attainment of postsecondary credentials as the surest path to opportunity, the college choice is decidedly a personal one. In *Choosing College*, Michael and Bob expertly apply the Jobs to Be Done theory to this seminal question, resulting in an incredibly relevant and useful guide for individuals, and those that support them, to evaluate their own reasons and purpose for attending college. It further highlights how and why different learners need different models and options to be successful. The research, personal stories, data, and conclusions weave a compelling narrative, whether you are a first-time, returning, or continuing learner.

Scott Pulsipher, president of Western Governors University

Michael B. Horn and Bob Moesta offer sensible and compassionate advice for students and parents alike. By reframing the college choice to focus on the actual reasons that people pursue a degree, *Choosing College* cuts through the mountains of rumor, hype, and sheer misinformation that typically surround this important decision. *Choosing College* is clear, concise, and well informed.

William Deresiewicz, author of Excellent Sheep

Choosing College

How To Make Better
Learning Decisions
Throughout Your Life

Michael B. Horn and Bob Moesta

JB JOSSEY-BASS™
A Wiley Brand

Published by Jossey-Bass
A Wiley Imprint
535 Mission St, 14th Floor; San Francisco CA 94105-3253—www.josseybass.com

Jossey-Bass books and products are available through most bookstores. To contact Jossey-Bass directly call our Customer Care Department within the U.S. at 800-956-7739, outside the U.S. at 317-572-3986, or fax 317-572-4002.

Wiley also publishes its books in a variety of electronic formats and by print-on-demand. Some material included with standard print versions of this book may not be included in e-books or in print-on-demand. If this book refers to media such as a CD or DVD that is not included in the version you purchased, you may download this material at http://booksupport.wiley.com. For more information about Wiley products, visit www.wiley.com.

Library of Congress Cataloging-in-Publication Data

Names: Horn, Michael B., author. | Moesta, Robert, 1964- author.
Title: Choosing college : How to make better learning decisions throughout your life / Michael B. Horn, Robert Moesta.
Description: First edition. | San Francisco, CA : Jossey-Bass, [2019] | Includes index.
Identifiers: LCCN 2019025696 (print) | LCCN 2019025697 (ebook) | ISBN 9781119570110 (hardback) | ISBN 9781119570165 (adobe pdf) | ISBN 9781119570134 (epub)
Subjects: LCSH: College choice. | Decision making. | College graduates—Employment. | Postsecondary education. | School-to-work transition.
Classification: LCC LB2350.5 .H632 2019 (print) | LCC LB2350.5 (ebook) | DDC 378.1/61—dc23
LC record available at https://lccn.loc.gov/2019025696
LC ebook record available at https://lccn.loc.gov/2019025697

Cover Design: Wiley
Cover Image: © NiseriN/Getty Images

Printed in the United States of America
FIRST EDITION
HB Printing   F10012473_073019

Contents

In Part II, we help you discover which Job describes your current context. To support that section, we built a tool that will help diagnose which of these Jobs you are experiencing right now. It's free with the purchase of this book. You can access it here: http://choosing.college.

Foreword: Helping You Make Progress

This book is about helping you make progress in your life. As you face struggles about whether or where to get more education, this book can help you figure out what you are trying to achieve. It then offers sound advice on how to get you there.

It builds off of work that I began with Bob Moesta over two decades ago at the Harvard Business School. Bob and his partner Rick Pedi brought me a puzzle around marketing and product development that has set us on a lifelong journey of collaboration. That puzzle was, "If a company offers a new service, how can it predict in advance whether a customer will buy it?" Even more interesting, can it predict whether a customer will be delighted by it?

Answering this question – along with many related ones – led to the development of the Jobs to Be Done theory. In a nutshell, people don't buy products or services simply because they fall into a particular demographic category. Rather, people *hire* services to get a job done in their lives so that they can make progress. Understanding this has helped us reframe the world from mere products, services, and categories – like "colleges," "universities," and "18- to 24-year-olds" – to understanding what *causes* people to make the choices they do. This has helped make innovation far more predictable.

Working as a professor at the Harvard Business School, where I have the opportunity to learn constantly from my students, has been one of life's greatest joys. Indeed, my students have helped Bob and I hone the Jobs to Be Done theory over the years to become even more precise and predictive.

My career in academia has also allowed me to have a close-up view of how much students could benefit from a clearer understanding of *why* they are going to school – or in our language – what Job they *hired* the school to get done in their lives. Too many students and families don't have a clear idea of why they are going to school, which leads them to make choices inconsistent with the progress they are seeking and their particular circumstances. It doesn't need to be this way.

Colleges and universities will also benefit from having a clearer sense of the "Job" they are being hired to do in the lives of students. Although colleges and universities delivered on a clear Job to Be Done in their infancy, as I've explored in some of my writing with Michael Horn, with whom I have collaborated on improving education for nearly 15 years now, they have evolved to be places that seek to do everything for everyone. As a result, most institutions don't do any given Job particularly well, and they've become much more expensive.

In reading *Choosing College*, I realized my former students – Bob and Michael – have once again taught me a tremendous amount. The book offers a clear, theory-driven approach for individuals and families making the college decision, as well as for higher education institutions as they decide where to focus in the future, a decision with existential ramifications.

Peeling back the layers for why you are doing something and then shedding light on the path ahead for what's next in your life is invaluable. I trust that you will find this book as useful as I do as I continue to learn and make progress in my own life.

Clayton M. Christensen
Harvard Business School

Part I

Introduction

Chapter 1

Is This Book for Me?

If you are thinking about whether you should get more education or where to get it, this book is for you.

But this book isn't your typical guide to schools. It's designed to help you better understand yourself and your current situation.

ASK THE RIGHT QUESTION

If you aren't currently considering more education, as you read you might learn that it's just what you need to make progress in your life. And if you're sure that more education is the right next step, you might surprise yourself and discover that it isn't.

Many books focus on the process of getting into school or how to rank different schools based on their features. This book doesn't tackle those questions.

Instead, if you are considering getting more education, this book will help you answer a more foundational question first. That question is *why?*

Why are you seeking more education in your life? Or why should you? What is the progress you are trying to make?

Once you know the answer, you will be ready to make a better choice – and making a good choice is more critical today than ever before, as the cost of college has risen and a mistake can be crippling, but the rewards can be life changing. In today's complex world of choosing college, you need every possible edge you can get.

If you're willing to put in just a little time and be honest with yourself, this book can give you that edge.

We've learned that there are many reasons people go back to school. And there are more people in situations just like yours than you could have ever imagined who are struggling just like you.

YOU COULD BE STRUGGLING BECAUSE ...

You are in high school and stressed out over the college admissions process.

You know exactly which college you want to attend, but understand that college admissions can be like a lottery and you aren't sure whether to apply to "safety" schools.

You feel that your parents, friends, family, school, or employer are pushing you to go to a school that doesn't excite you.

You feel like you're just going through the motions as you apply and that education is the next logical step in your life.

You're unsure whether college – or any education at all – is the right next step.

You feel stuck – at home, in your town, in your job, or in a relationship – and that going to school would provide a good escape.

You are in a rut at work, know what you want next, and understand that you need more education to get there.

You are in a rut at work, don't know what you want next, and think education could help you figure it out.

You're ready to take the next step in your career and know what education you need to get there.

You are late in your career and wish you had pursued a dream earlier through more education.

You are at a comfortable place in your life and ready to learn more.

You have been out of the workforce, want to get back in, and think going back to school could help.

In all of these situations and many others, you have a struggle. You're trying to figure out what's next. And we can help you.

WHY THIS BOOK CAN HELP

This book can help by giving you the language to understand the outcome you are seeking in your situation. It will also give those around you, like your parents, the language to understand what you are going through so they communicate on your terms, not theirs.

How? Because we interviewed and interrogated people to collect more than 200 detailed stories of individuals making choices just like yours. And then we surveyed well over a 1000 more students to learn about their choosing process, too.

We didn't collect stories from just anybody. We collected them from people resembling nearly everybody.

We talked to people who chose four-year schools, two-year schools, coding bootcamps, online schools, and more. We interviewed women and men of all races. We talked to students who were under 18 all the way up to students who were over 60. Some of the students we talked to already had a college or even a master's or PhD degree. Others had only a high school diploma or a General Educational Diploma (GED). Some were the first in their family to go to college. We talked to both students who attended school full-time, as well as those who worked while they attended. The students we talked to came from wealthy, middle-class, and low-income families.

The one thing they had in common? They were choosing whether and where to get more education.

We didn't just collect their stories. Once we had them, we analyzed them to learn *why* people were choosing school. We discovered what was driving each person to seek more education and what success in each situation looked like – what we call a "Job to Be Done."

We discovered that there are *five* "Jobs to Be Done" for which people choose college. That's right. After collecting over 200 stories and surveying well over a thousand students, we found just five *Jobs*.

People choose school to:

1. Get into "their best" school
2. Do what's expected of them
3. Get away
4. Step it up
5. Extend themselves

Sounds simple, right? Well, it is … and isn't.

Each "Job" is filled with lots of underlying forces and reasons that shape people's decisions.

Some of these reasons are functional considerations. For example, if I get another degree, I'll get a raise that justifies the cost.

But we're not robots. We typically don't do things just for functional reasons. More often than not, the forces acting on us are emotional or social. For example, all of my friends are going to college, so maybe I should, too. Or, I really want to challenge myself to see if I can do this.

After all, the choice to get more education – or where to get that education – is complicated.

There are many forces tugging on us in all directions. We are pushed and pulled by our dreams and aspirations, by what people in our lives tell us and do, by society's expectations, and by basic needs. From a young age, some just assume they will go to college after high school. Others don't think of college until much later. For many of us, our decisions are anchored early on by sports allegiances, family ties and stories, formative educational experiences, geographic considerations, financial matters, and more.[1]

But you already know that, or you wouldn't be reading this book.

That's why we call your motivations for going to college "Jobs" rather than just "reasons" or some other name. A "Job" captures the *set* of reasons that *cause* you to do something, along with your circumstances and a clear understanding of what success looks like in that context. *In the book, we capitalize the word "Job" whenever we are referring to a "Job to Be Done" to avoid confusion from the everyday usage of the word "job" – a paid position of employment – which many suggest is the primary reason people go to college today (spoiler alert: it's more complicated than that).*

Bob Moesta, one of this book's coauthors, created the Jobs to Be Done theory. It is more than just theoretical. Understanding human behavior – what people actually do, not just what they say they will do – can help people make better choices.

Bob developed his theory more than two decades ago with Harvard Business School Professor Clayton Christensen, and he's used it to build over 3500 new services, products, and businesses across nearly every industry – not only for education, but also for cars, consumer packaged goods, food, defense, software, financial services, and health care. The services and products that Bob and his team at the ReWired Group have helped develop account for billions of dollars of sales per year. The central insight behind the theory is that people don't buy products or services for their own sake. Instead, they "hire" products and services to help them do a Job – which is to say, make progress in a specific circumstance in their life.

Pairing Bob with Michael Horn, the other author of this book, who for over a decade has been researching, writing about, and shaping the future of education, as well as helping students and schools innovate, allowed us to uncover insights to help *you*.

HELPING YOU AS A STUDENT

And that's where we start. In the next chapter, we tell you why now, more than ever before, getting the college-choosing process right is so important.

Part II of the book is then focused on helping you make a good decision given your situation. In Chapters 3–7, we explore each Job to help you discover which one describes your current context. To help you identify which Job you're in right now, we share several of the stories from the people we talked to so that the Jobs are clear and concrete. **We also built a tool that will help diagnose which of these Jobs you are experiencing right now. It's free with the purchase of this book. You can download it at http://choosing.college.**

For each Job we then offer advice for how to be successful. But more importantly, we offer guardrails to help you avoid a misstep.

Our advice is based on what we learned from the specific examples and patterns that emerged from the people we interviewed, as well as external research, our experience in designing new services to help people accomplish their Jobs, and our own personal experiences. Given that this is the first time we are publishing this research, we are sure that our advice is not comprehensive. Once you know what circumstance applies to you, you should talk with your friends and family.

To help you do so, the advice is structured in three steps in each chapter so you can walk through a design process and build a Job to Be Done profile for yourself:

> **Step 1: Know thyself.** In this step, you clarify your current situation and what's important to you right now from a functional, emotional, and social perspective.

> **Step 2: Identify matches.** Here, you identify what educational options you can potentially hire to help you accomplish your Job based on the experiences you must have to help you make progress.

Step 3: Check and choose. In this step, you try out different solutions to learn precisely where you need to make progress – and importantly, what won't work – and then you make your choice.

The goal is to help you make a better decision and get more value out of any education you pursue after high school – ranging from college to a short online course, or law school to a coding bootcamp.

Then we put it all together in Chapter 8 so you can see how, over the course of your life, you're likely to experience most, if not all, of these Jobs – some of them several times – and what that means for you.

This book won't give you "the answer" – as if there is only one – of where to go to school. We won't break down the minutiae of every aspect of college, from cost to scholarships and from accessibility of faculty and teaching assistants to college safety. Other books, guides, and tools can help with that – but only once you know why you are going and what you're really chasing.

Part II will help you figure that out, along with Chapter 11 in Part IV at the end of the book that summarizes three key insights for you.

HELPING YOU AS A PARENT

If you're a parent, Part II is also for you. Perhaps the only thing more nerve-wracking than figuring out what is next in your own life is wondering what is next for your child.

This book will help you with both. And even it will give you the language to be able to talk to your child in *their* language so that you can better understand each other and not talk past one another. If you have already completed college, you will continue to learn throughout your life, so *each of the Jobs will have direct relevance for you.* That's right – as you read, you're likely to realize that this book will help you in your own life journey, not just your child's.

But at the end of each of the chapters in which we explore a Job we discovered (Chapters 3–7), we offer you concrete advice as a parent. The advice is aimed so you can help your child make progress given her goals – not yours – and so you don't set her back.

The insights and recommendations in these sections will also help guidance counselors, college counselors, and high school educators, as well as friends and colleagues of people struggling with the question of whether and where to pursue more education. Although we don't dive into the question of how high schools should redesign themselves based on what we've learned in this book, there is no question that there are many redesign opportunities to better prepare students for the journey of learning throughout their lives.[2]

HELPING YOU AS A SCHOOL PROFESSIONAL

This book isn't just for helping prospective students and parents. Helping students make better choices will force schools to improve. But we also want to help schools improve directly so they can innovate and offer better choices to students.

If you work at a college or university, lead or work at another type of educational program, or plan on starting one, Part II will help you understand why students consider and enroll in your school. That's the demand side of the equation.

Part III focuses on the supply side. It shows you how to design your school to help students be successful in their educational journeys. If you're a student or parent, reading Part III will help you know what to look for to see if schools are acting with your Job in mind. Not including this section would be doing an injustice because we'd be shortchanging one half of the equation that can improve the education choices you have available. But if you're a student or parent, Part III is *not* required reading.

If you work at an education provider, we dive deeper into the Jobs to Be Done theory in Chapter 9 so you can see why understanding the Job to Be Done affects both how you design your service and structure your organization to maximize the odds of success and efficiency. We also offer guardrails to help you avoid offering a one-size-fits-none solution.

In Chapter 10, we provide some insights into how to design better experiences for each of the different Jobs. We do not have all the answers, but in some cases, we recommend some radical restructuring to help students accomplish their goals given the circumstances in which they find themselves hiring education.

In Part IV, Chapter 11 summarizes and expands on some of the big insights that emerged in the course of the book. We also offer an Appendix that explains our research process – how you discover a Job to Be Done, how we found people to interview, and whom we interviewed. You only have to read the Appendix if you are interested in doing Jobs to Be Done research yourself or want to better understand our methodology.

So let's get started. A world of better decisions about your educational choices awaits you.

Chapter 2

College Choosers Face a New, High-Stakes World

THE COLLEGE-CHOOSING PROBLEM

In the United States, we have a college-choosing problem.

The problem isn't limited to what we think of as college. It's much bigger. All of us struggle to make choices about *postsecondary education* – or education after high school. If you are currently struggling to figure out whether to pursue more education or where to seek it, you are not alone.

You might be saying, "Sure, but haven't we always had a college-choosing problem? It's such an important decision!"

Maybe. But it's different and more complicated now.[1] For most students, it's higher stakes. A mistake can have serious consequences. That's why understanding why you're going and what you hope to get out of the experience is so important.

Focusing on college is an easy place to see the problem of choosing any education after high school and how it's changed over time.

A HIGHER PERCENTAGE OF PEOPLE ARE GOING TO COLLEGE THAN EVER BEFORE

Over 3 million high school seniors say they plan to go to college each year. More than 2 million do.[2] That's roughly 70% of high school graduates.[3]

A generation ago, approximately 1.5 million high school graduates attended college – or 60%. A generation before that? Just 750 000 high school graduates went to college – about 45%.[4]

It's true that the total number of people going to college has declined some in the last few years. The number may continue to fall modestly in the years ahead. How do we know? Because birth rates in the United States have declined, which means there will be fewer high school students in the years to come. But even after accounting for that fact, 5 million more students are enrolled in accredited colleges and universities today than 20 years ago.

MORE PEOPLE APPLY TO MORE PLACES

Some students obsess over the college-choosing process. They spend months applying to multiple colleges and anguish as they choose which school to attend. Their process starts at least as early as their freshman year of high school.

They visit multiple colleges, invest in high-priced tutoring for the SAT or ACT,[5] pay for college counselors to help prepare their college applications, and overprogram themselves with extracurricular activities.

You might fit into this group. One student we interviewed, Kolby, did.

Kolby's real name and other details about his story are disguised so as to preserve the real student's anonymity. We employ this practice throughout the book.

Kolby took the PSAT – a standardized test that roughly 3.5 million students take each year to try and get recognition from the National Merit Scholarship program. He did well. When his scores came back, he was invited to attend three conferences, each showcasing five colleges. At one of the conferences he fell in love with one of the schools.

But he didn't stop his college-choosing process there. He visited 18 colleges as he decided where to apply. He ended up applying to 8, including the school he had fallen in love with at the conference that was prestigious, ranked highly, and focused on undergraduates. He loved that it was outside the glare of a city, tucked away in a remote part of the country. The campus was close-knit and picturesque. Its study abroad and language-learning programs were unparalleled, Kolby said.

He did everything he could to get in. He did not sign up for Junior ROTC, an interest of his, because it would count as a class and lower his weighted grade point average (GPA). He signed up for Model United

Nations because he thought it would make him look more attractive. His mother was part Native American, but he lacked the official recognition, so he worked to change that so he would have a leg up as an ethnic minority. As he looked at his grades and extracurricular activities, Kolby felt sure he would get in everywhere he applied.

The group of students like Kolby is growing. In 1990, just 9% of students applied to 7 or more colleges. By 2016, 35% did.[6] A subset of students applies to 20, 30, or even 50 schools.[7] The stress of the choosing process is overwhelming.

MANY DON'T KNOW WHETHER TO GO TO COLLEGE AT ALL

Millions of students struggle through a different decision: whether to go to college at all.

Maybe this describes you. It described J. D. Vance, who wrote the best-selling book *Hillbilly Elegy*.

In his book, Vance details the excruciating work of deciphering Ohio State's financial aid package with its "talk of Pell Grants, subsidized loans, unsubsidized loans, scholarships, and something called 'work-study.'" Actually filling out the forms would require "another Herculean effort." Vance's "excitement turned to apprehension" as he began to worry whether he was even ready for college. As he wrote, "Not all investments are good investments."[8]

WANT A JOB? GO TO COLLEGE!

Against that backdrop, the pressure to go to college is higher than it's ever been.

Society says you must go. In his first major speech to Congress, President Barack Obama called on every American to "commit" to attending at least one year of college so that "America will once again have the highest proportion of college graduates in the world."[9]

And if you want to get a good job, the statistics say that, on average, you should go to college.

When manufacturing jobs disappeared in the United States in the early 1980s and technology started remaking every part of our economy, that "essentially mandated education after high school," Jeff Selingo wrote in *There Is Life after College*.

If you graduated college with a bachelor's degree in the 1970s, your lifetime earnings were less than 40% higher than someone with just a high school diploma.

Today? Even after a small decline over the past few years, someone who graduates from college with a bachelor's degree will earn at least 80% more on average than someone who didn't. That means college graduates can expect to earn roughly 1 million dollars more than high school graduates over their lifetimes. That's a strong investment.[10]

But college costs have gone up significantly. Does the amount of money you make justify paying for college?

On average, yes.

Studies that account for the benefits *and* costs of college conclude that the investment is worth it. In 1970, the rate of return of a bachelor's degree was roughly 8%. According to the Federal Reserve Bank of New York, it now hovers around 14%.[11]

The unemployment rate also suggests the advantages of having a degree. In 2014, bachelor's degree holders had a 3.5% unemployment rate. Americans with only a high school diploma had a 6% unemployment rate.[12]

Here's the bottom line. In the 1960s and 1970s, you could land a good-paying job after high school, the military, apprenticing, or college. But then manufacturing jobs dried up, and until recently, society told us that we had only two options: college or the military – and less than 1% of Americans serve in the military. In some quarters, people are beginning to encourage career technical education, but the dominant narrative still emphasizes college as the best option for financial success.[13]

STOP STRESSING ABOUT WHETHER YOU'LL GET IN

Here's the dirty secret.

If your goal is to get into college, you will get in. Fewer than 100 colleges are highly selective, which means they accept less than 25% of applicants. Nearly 500 four-year colleges accept more than 75% of applicants. There are also open-admissions colleges that accept nearly everyone who graduates high school.[14]

As Frank Bruni documents in his best-selling book *Where You Go Is Not Who You'll Be*, if you go to a nonselective school, build a strong network, and work hard – while in college or afterward – you can do more than just fine. You can become a leader in your field. John Katzman, the founder of such education companies as Noodle and the Princeton Review, even points out that although it is harder than ever to get into a specific top 10 school today, collectively speaking, it's statistically easier to get into one of the top 50 schools today than it was 30 years ago.[15]

It's not worth stressing about whether you will get into a school.

COLLEGE DOESN'T WORK FOR MANY PEOPLE

Whether you choose the right school or whether you should attend right now is a different matter.

Despite college's benefits on average, you aren't "average." No one is. The reality is this: College does not work for many. It might not work for you right now.

Forty-two percent of students fail to graduate from four-year programs within six years. You read that right – 42%!

It's worse at two-year colleges, where only 26% complete.[16] Of those entering community colleges, 80% expect to transfer and earn a bachelor's degree. Only 17% do so within six years, however, according to the National Student Clearinghouse Research Center.[17]

If you are in the top-income quartile, you're more likely to graduate – 77% do. But that means nearly a quarter of relatively well-off students don't graduate. And it's worse if you are in the bottom-income quartile. Way worse. The graduation rate is 11%.

And not all colleges are created equal. Out of 535 four-year public institutions, for example, only 15% of them – 80 in total – graduate more than two-thirds of their first-time, full-time students each year.[18] That means that at more than 450 state four-year colleges and universities, over a third of students don't graduate.

All of that means that today, nearly 37 million Americans – more than one-fifth of the working-age population – have attended some college but have no degree to show for it.[19]

COLLEGE DOESN'T PAY OFF FOR MANY PEOPLE

There are many reasons why students don't complete college. As college became the pathway to success and enrollments surged in the 1970s, dropouts surged, too, because colleges admitted many who were unprepared academically, were poor fits, or had complicated lives that made sticking with college difficult, whether for work, financial, health, or family reasons. Although there are exceptions like Steve Jobs, Bill Gates, or Mark Zuckerberg, you generally don't want to be one of those students. Especially these days.

Why? Because college is more expensive than ever.

The average sticker price of a private college has soared – from 20% of the median family income in the 1980s to 40% in 2002 and a staggering 55% in 2012. Even at public colleges, the average sticker price has soared from 5% of the median family income in the 1980s to 16% in 2012.[20]

Now you might say, but with grants, scholarships and other financial aid, has it really risen that fast? The answer is no, but even when you account for those things – what people call *net tuition* – the price tag has still gone up. Way up.

After accounting for all the forms of aid and the average price students and families actually pay, the price of college rose 92% when accounting for inflation from 1987 to 2010.[21] That is, the price of getting a college education almost doubled.

What's more, it's hard to know ahead of time how much you will pay, even if you come from a family of limited means. The New America Foundation, a think tank in Washington, DC, studied 479 private colleges. It found that a whopping 61% of them were charging $15 000 or more per year to students from families with incomes of $30 000 or less, even after taking into account all federal, state, and institutional aid the students received.[22]

Even more misleading, many colleges tack on a variety of fees to the tuition bill, from a $130 Sports Pass at Boston University to an annual capital projects fee of $1470 at Fitchburg State University. From 2000 to 2017, fees at public universities increased 100% – meaning they doubled in just 17 years – while tuition increased 80%, according to Robert Kelchen, an assistant professor at Seton Hall University.[23]

The price of traditional college is likely to keep rising, as the costs underlying college continue to increase.

So if you go to college, unless you're offered a great opportunity midway through, make sure you complete it. Because if you pay for some college and don't graduate, it can be costly.

Students who take out loans but don't complete are often worse off than if they had never enrolled in the first place. Americans in this camp have a tiny bump in wages over those with a high school diploma, but they have the same unemployment rate as Americans with just a high school diploma.[24] And the debt you assume – even if it sounds modest – is likely to be a significant chunk of your earnings.[25]

Given the relatively high payoff to completing college, that might be an acceptable risk if the cost of college was not so high. But that's no longer the case.

Paying $2 to play the lottery a couple times a year has very little downside and potentially a big upside. Going to college isn't the same equation. Although the upside is more certain at college than in the lottery, the cost of college is high, which means a much bigger downside.

Because incomes across America have stagnated in recent years and the returns from college have declined slightly in the last few years,[26] the cost of failure is higher than ever, so you have to get it right.

EVEN IF YOU COMPLETE, IT MIGHT NOT BE A GOOD INVESTMENT

And that's the dirtier secret. Even if you complete, the college degree isn't what it used to be.

Recent graduates under 25 suffered a 9% unemployment rate during the Great Recession.[27]

According to Burning Glass Technologies and the Strada Institute for the Future of Work, two groups that research jobs and education, 43% of new graduates were *underemployed* in their first job. That means that they worked in a job that did not require the degree they had earned.

That might not be so bad. Many of us have taken odd jobs after college, right? But Burning Glass and Strada looked deeper and learned that if you are underemployed in your first job, there is also a good chance you will remain underemployed 5 and 10 years later. That equates to a loss in salary of roughly $10 000 per year.[28]

THERE ARE OTHER GOOD PATHWAYS

You don't have to go to college to live a good life. Not right away, certainly.

Some Americans find other pathways that out-earn someone with a bachelor's degree. For example, the Georgetown Center on Workforce Development has shown that in some fields, those with associate degrees "out-earn 28% of those with bachelor's degrees." In fields like computing and information services, those who attain low-cost certificates can out-earn people with pricier bachelor's degrees.[29] Companies such as Google, Apple, IBM, and Bank of America no longer require a college degree for many job openings.[30]

THAT ADDS UP TO A LOT OF DISSATISFIED PEOPLE

At best, choosing college is a satisfying process for a precious few.

Although millions love their college experience, benefit from the high payoff of a degree, and get the final decision right – or at least right enough – many millions do not.

According to Gallup and the Strada Education Network, 51% of Americans would change something about their college education – their major, institution, or degree.[31]

Going back to Kolby's story, after he applied to eight schools, he fell into this group. What became of his dream college? It rejected Kolby. "It was like I had had a midlife crisis," he told us. "I was so very convinced that my life was ruined."

His second choice also rejected him. So did two other schools.

Kolby didn't get rejected from everywhere, though. Four schools accepted him, but none of them excited him.

Three were too expensive, despite his efforts to qualify for financial aid, he said. The fourth school, his state's flagship university, felt like the wrong fit from top to bottom. It was in a city. It didn't have the language and study-abroad programs he wanted. And it didn't have the prestige of his dream school.

Kolby considered enlisting in the military instead. He talked to military recruiters from four branches of the military. The Air Force and Navy both appealed to him. But when he broached the topic with his mom, she was mortified. She strongly discouraged him. She – along with her entire side of the family – could not believe he would skip college.

With his parents insisting he go to college for at least a year, Kolby relented. He begrudgingly enrolled in his state's flagship university. And he ended up despising the experience.

Even as college may be a wise choice on average, no student is average. Each sits in her own circumstance trying to make progress in her life. Making a choice that is not a good fit or when you are not ready to make the commitment is a problem.

IT'S NOT JUST 18-YEAR-OLD HIGH SCHOOL GRADUATES

That problem is not just limited to 18-year-olds choosing whether to attend college or which college to attend. Millions of adults attend colleges and universities, too. They also struggle to graduate.

As the high school population shrinks in the next few years and the pace of technological change increases, many of us will need to reskill far more frequently. Both the percentage and total number of adults enrolled in postsecondary education will likely rise. Today, roughly 40% of students at accredited colleges and universities are older than 25.[32]

Perhaps you are one of them.

Mindy was. She tried college twice before she was 20. Both times she dropped out. At the second college, she had at least enrolled in a program that matched her career interest of becoming a midwife. But the program's approach to midwifery did not resonate with her, so she quit.

Rather than try school again, Mindy began working in a big-box retail store. She started climbing the career ladder and was on track to become a manager, but then her mom was diagnosed with cancer. Mindy moved to be close to her and transferred stores. She soon realized that the new retail store was not the right fit. She butted heads with its management. So she quit to support her mom's care.

After a month of unemployment, Mindy got the itch to step it up and try college again as she neared her 30s. But she was nervous. She remained interested in becoming a midwife, but she felt she had to settle for whatever school would take her.

As luck would have it, she stumbled upon an online college with a national reputation and a teaching program. She had a hunch it would accept her, so she applied.

Her aunt and many of her cousins were teachers. Mindy rationalized that teaching might be a good backup career option.

When she was accepted, she enrolled immediately, even though she felt she was settling. "I thought my standards were too high, and I didn't have any faith in myself," she said.

She figured that if she showed that she could hang on in college but did not want to become a teacher, then once in the school she could change programs and enter a track that would help her become a midwife. But she had to prove to herself that she was college material.

Should Mindy have enrolled? She knew that a college degree could help her for all the reasons we've described. But within a month, she decided that teaching was not for her. Only then did she discover that the college did not have any programs that offered a way to become a midwife. She was stuck yet again – so yet again she dropped out.

Despite having the advantages of experience and, in some cases, friends who have completed college, adults aren't necessarily wiser when it comes to choosing college. Students like Mindy who have attended college at least once before have a significantly lower graduation rate than first-time college goers.[33] They have the college-choosing problem, too.

That problem isn't limited to choosing among accredited colleges and universities. Students' education choices are exploding.

Would-be students today have a more complicated decision, as they must navigate everything from coding bootcamps to short technical training programs that teach programming skills to help students get jobs, and from online courses to a range of local community experiences. That's on top of the range of accredited colleges and universities.

THE RANKINGS AND ADVICE OUT THERE WON'T NECESSARILY HELP YOU

The rankings, metrics, analytics, tools, college visits, and well-meaning advice and recommendations from family, friends, counselors, and teachers to help you make these decisions are likely out of step with the progress you are trying to make.

Many surveys increasingly say that people go to college to get a job – nearly 90%, according to UCLA's annual survey of freshmen entering four-year colleges and universities. That is up from roughly two-thirds in the mid-1970s.

But our research shows that it is more complicated than that. A simple survey simply misses the complexity of what's driving your choice. Instead of surveying people, we watched what they actually did. We saw what they actually prioritized, not what they said was important.

As you delve into the chapters ahead to help you understand why you are seeking more college, you'll see that "searching for a job" may be part of your why, but it's far from the dominant reason so-called experts say it is.

With little college experience surrounding them, students who are the first to attend college in their families have an even more challenging decision to make. But even if your parents attended college, their advice is based on outdated experiences from 30 years ago. A lot has changed since then. We often lament how students don't know what they don't know, but we as parents don't know what we don't know, either.

None of the tools today give you the information and context you need to make such a high-stakes decision about what to do next. As we'll see, if you're going to college to get away, for example, the criteria for your decision are dramatically different from someone who is going for other reasons. The definition of success is different, depending on which "Job to Be Done" you have.

DON'T LEAVE YOUR CHOICE TO LUCK

Although it is easy to see whether someone has made the right education choice after the fact, for many, choosing college is too big a decision to be left to hindsight or luck.

We do not get many cracks at making high-stakes choices. College is often your first chance. No one wants to be like Kolby or Mindy.

Even as the stakes attached to choosing college have soared to the point where it can be hard to recover from a bad choice, the process for choosing has unfortunately largely stayed the same.

This book aims to change that by preparing you to understand the real decision you face. It makes the unconscious conscious.

How? By helping you understand what "Job" you are "hiring" school to do for you.

To review, we uncovered five Jobs for which people hire postsecondary education in our research. To preview the Jobs, people hire postsecondary education to help them:

1. **Get into their best school.** The students in this Job typically want the classic college experience with the beautiful campus and prestigious brand-name school so they can reinvent themselves with new people, but they have rarely thought about what they will do once enrolled. For them, making progress is all about getting accepted.

2. **Do what's expected of them.** Students experiencing this Job are going to satisfy or obey someone else in their lives, often when they have a dream school that they didn't get into. They are looking to check a box with a degree, don't see other options besides schooling, and feel that school is the next logical step in their lives that will give them a safety net to fall back on.

3. **Get away.** The students with this Job are looking to get away from their day job; break a current habit; or leave home and their family, town, or a particular relationship, and they are looking to go to a place where they will know a supportive person and to check a box with a degree.

4. **Step it up.** Students in this Job turn to school when they don't recognize themselves in some part of their life – they want to get away from their current place of employment, role, or habit – and are ready to step it up and do better. They typically feel like time is running out, and they are afraid of where things are headed unless they take action. They know that specific, practical skills or certifications will help them get back on track.

5. **Extend themselves.** Students with this Job are looking to learn more and challenge themselves so they can pursue a clear vision and get some practical skills or certifications. Life is good, and they now have the time to pursue this vision.

In the chapters ahead, we help you figure out which Job you are experiencing *right now*. In the course of your life, you will experience most, if not all, of these Jobs.

Armed with the knowledge of which Job you are experiencing and the advice and guardrails we provide, you can clearly frame the options before you – and see options you never knew you had. It's true that not all decisions regarding getting more education will be high stakes. But it is critical to know in advance when one is or isn't and the resulting implications.

That's because the college-choosing problem – and the problem of choosing education throughout our adult lives – is never-ending. To make the best choice for you – whether that is college or a lower-risk option – it is critical that you identify your current Job to Be Done.

That's where the next chapter starts – by exploring the Help Me Get into My Best School Job – over which millions of dollars' worth of magazines, books, and rankings guides are sold each year.

Part II

Helping Learners Make Better Choices

Chapter 3

Help Me Get into My Best School

If you are looking to take the next logical step in your life by:

- Having the classic "college experience";
- Living in a brick-and-mortar college;
- Belonging to a place with prestige and a great reputation;
- And/or reinventing yourself and meeting new people

Then the Job you have right now is what we call Help Me Get into My Best School.

GETTING IN

The process of getting into your best school is the Job that is glamorized in Hollywood and worried about in the pages of the *New York Times*. It is the Job that sparked the interest of major media outlets in early 2019 when several celebrities, among others, were charged with illegally cheating to get their children into the best schools.[1] Some families spend lots of money on college counselors. Some hire testing coaches. Some make huge donations. Some game the system and use all of these options. The factors in how exactly students get into the best schools are the focus of much of the country's admissions mania.

Contrary to what you might think, you don't have to be stressed out to be experiencing this Job or about to graduate high school. It can occur multiple times in your life, from college to graduate school and other exclusive experiences. In the latter cases, you probably identify with the statements about belonging to a place with prestige and reinventing yourself but not about having the classic "college experience" or living in a brick-and-mortar college.

This Job is all about the act of getting *into* school, less on what you will do *after* you get in to the school. That makes it strange as a Job to Be Done because the outcome that people desire is more the affirmation from getting into school, not the schooling experience itself or the doors that college may open for you.

Sure, you might be going into school as a pre-med student or to get employed "in business." You might have a sense of the classes you'll take, the parties you might attend, and the fun you might have. But deep down, the emphasis is all about *getting in* and getting the best *for you.* What you will do once you're in and why you are going are typically not so concrete.

As Frank Bruni wrote in *Where You Go Is Not Who You'll Be,* "How you use college. What you demand of it. These dynamics get lost in the admissions mania, which overshadows them, to a point where it makes them seem close to irrelevant."[2]

We thought of calling this Job "Help me execute 'the plan,'" but the students we talked to don't typically use that language, even as some of their parents might. The students don't always have a plan, more just a yearning to get into "the best." These are the students who excel "at getting into things," Bruni wrote. "The message these kids had received from the college admissions mania was that gaining access, besting the competition, was the principal goal and primary accomplishment. You rallied your best self, or struck your comeliest pose, for that. You didn't worry as much about what came after."[3]

Our research shows that students with this Job are overwhelmingly satisfied with their experience – 83%. Just 28% of students dropped out or transferred schools.

Despite that track record of success, if you are experiencing this Job there are some pitfalls to avoid. There are also some steps to consider ahead of time because once you get in, the next step is going to school. For many students, that moves them into a new Job. It's wise to be ready for that potential pivot ahead of time.

But before we detail that, we explore this Job more in-depth. We start with three stories of people who experienced it to help you see if this Job matches where you are right now.

DEVIN'S STORY

Devin bled burnt orange. For as long as he could remember, he rooted for the University of Texas at Austin (UT-Austin) Longhorns. When the school's football team played on Saturdays, his family always tuned in to watch on TV. Although his family, which lived in Dallas, was interested in the games, Devin could not get enough of them. He wore Longhorn paraphernalia everywhere.

An athlete in high school – he played on his school's varsity baseball team – Devin briefly considered applying to small colleges where he could continue playing baseball. But he knew baseball wasn't going to figure into his career plans. He was a good athlete, but not an elite one. Making a decision just so he could continue to play the game he loved did not make much sense. After all, he said, his grandmother had told him that when she was working as a recruiter on behalf of companies, she liked to hire employees that had attended certain colleges that had some prestige. Where he went to college would matter for his future career options.

A strong student, Devin's GPA was always ranked near the top of his high school class of roughly 460 students. He had not given much thought to college the first couple of years of high school. He figured he would stay in state and go to a public college that was affordable, but he also assumed that the private colleges in the state were the top ones. It stood to reason that if you paid more, the education was better, he said.

When his junior year started, he began researching different colleges. To his surprise, he learned that UT-Austin was highly regarded for its academics, not just its athletics. The decision felt sealed then. If he could stay in the top 7%

of his high school class, he would gain automatic admittance to UT-Austin. He could attend and double down on his Longhorn pride.

Devin did better than the top 7%. He stayed in the top 5% of his class. He applied to UT-Austin in October. While he waited to hear back, he started an application to another public school in the state in case something unexpected happened. But when he heard from UT-Austin that he had been accepted a short time later, he was thrilled and stopped the other application. He would be a Longhorn.

TALIKHA'S STORY

The daughter of parents who both graduated from college, Talikha always assumed she would enroll in college after graduating high school. Growing up in California, she attended a prestigious all-girls high school and hoped that she would be able to attend college out-of-state.

By her sophomore year, Talikha had worked with the counselors at her school to create a first draft list of colleges she would apply to. When senior year rolled around, she applied to 22 schools all over the country. She was accepted to 19 of them and wait-listed at 2 more, where she ultimately got in as well.

With a desire to pursue degrees that would prepare her for the business world and a possible career in the technology industry, Talikha narrowed her list to five schools located across the country. She visited all five over a two-week period in April and said that being on-campus was really important for picking up the vibe of the place.

She ruled out a few because the location didn't feel enough like home, she said. She started to home in on a public flagship university outside of California because the vibe in the town felt right with a strong active business and entrepreneurial sector in a hopping urban environment. The business school was highly ranked at the university, which fueled her interest. And she had the opportunity to meet with advisors and professors while on campus. That she could receive such personal attention at a big school made an impression on her. She followed up by contacting alumni of the college's business school through LinkedIn and talked to them on the phone. They gave glowing reviews and spoke about all the opportunities to learn skills like networking through various clubs outside the classroom, which further excited her.

Shortly after, she made the decision to attend. She admitted that despite looking into schools that would prepare her for a career in business and technology, she had little sense for what she would do next – graduate school or work but was excited for the journey ahead.

UJANA'S STORY

Ujana was a talented singer. She qualified for the all-regional choir as a sophomore, which allowed her to join a special choir at her high school that took part in competitions around the country. In addition to her singing, she also continued piano lessons during high school.

During her junior year, her piano teacher recommended Ujana look into a nearby historically black college where her teacher knew the choir director. Her piano teacher told Ujana that she might be able to get a merit scholarship on the strength of her singing to attend the college and sing in its gospel choir. She helped Ujana understand the process to get in and what she would need to do to prepare. Around the same time, Ujana's sister, who was one year older and close with Ujana, got into that very college on a full-ride scholarship because of her voice.

As senior year dawned, Ujana's high school choir director pulled her aside to suggest she start preparing to audition for college choirs. Tryouts for most were in January, and it would take two to three months to learn the music.

Ujana also worked with her guidance counselor to create a list of colleges to apply to. She attended a college fair and thought through different options. She wanted something nearby to be close to family, and she wanted the school to have a good choir with small class sizes and nice dorms. She also wanted it to have a strong early childhood program, as at the beginning of her freshman year a career counselor at her high school had helped her figure out that she likely wanted to become a daycare employee or an elementary school teacher like her Mom, who had started teaching a few years earlier.

She narrowed her list to five schools, including the historically black college where her sister attended, as well as one other historically black college that also had a strong gospel choir. The other schools had choirs about which she was not particularly excited, but she applied to all five anyway.

Soon thereafter, her sister's choir came to her hometown. Ujana heard them perform for the first time. She was struck by the music they sang. It was not just one genre of gospel, but a variety. They also seemed disciplined and professional. When she met the choir director, he told her how she would have to seriously prepare for the tryouts. Then her piano teacher and sister both introduced her to the whole choir, which took her in "like a family," she said. It left her with a nice warm feeling, and she had her heart set.

She prepared accordingly and passed the first tryout. It was then that she got to hear the other historically black college's choir. She was not as impressed. She shared a meal with the choir members, and the magic feeling of family she had felt with her sister's choir was absent.

When the school where her sister attended accepted Ujana and offered her a full scholarship, her decision was made. She called the choir director to inform him that she would enroll in the fall. She then began practicing three times a day over the summer to prepare for the gospel choir auditions for when she arrived on campus.

UNDERSTANDING THE HELP ME GET INTO MY BEST SCHOOL JOB

If you are like Devin, Talikha, and Ujana, then your current reality is going away. You are in your senior year of high school and will be graduating soon. Or perhaps you are finishing up college, the military, or the last year of a two-year job.

School feels like the next logical step. Devin, Talikha, and Ujana never questioned whether they would apply and go to college. One student we talked to, Lawrence, said he had always known he would go to college. But growing up in a low-income family as the son of parents who had not gone to college, Lawrence said he spent his four years in high school "thinking of ways to not go into debt.... And the only thing that came to mind – unless I won a lottery – was going into the military." When his four years of service in the Marines were up, school was the next step.

- If you are experiencing this Job, the idea of college is probably alluring for its own sake.
- The students we talked to typically wanted attractive, comfortable, and lively brick-and-mortar schools.
- They cared about prestige. Rankings mattered.
- And many looked forward to starting in a new town with a new group of people and were excited to "reinvent" themselves.

Despite what you might answer on a survey about wanting to get a paid job after college, if you are experiencing this Job to be Done, deep down the outcome you desire is more about getting into college. In contrast to the other Jobs we will explore, it's less about what college will help you do or attain. Although getting access to a network and work opportunities could be bundled in to your sense of what "best" for you means,[4] most experiencing this Job to Be Done have little real understanding of what "work" will mean.

Devin factored in his grandmother's words about the importance of college for landing a good-paying job, but choosing a place based on a future career was not his prime factor. He needed a place that was good enough in his mind. Once the University of Texas cleared that basic hurdle, seeing it as his top college choice was a no brainer. Ujana was interested in working with children, but it was not the main driver for choosing her school. Talikha wanted to go to a school that would prepare her for a career in business and technology, but she admitted that she had little sense for what she would do after she graduated.

This lack of understanding of what might occur after college helps explain why many default to being a "business" major with the idea of taking a job "in business" nationwide. Although there are some exceptions – like for some who enter college with the intention of becoming a doctor – even the apparent exceptions are often mostly focused on climbing the ladder and getting into the "best" school for them.

That last clause – "for them" – is important. This Job is about being the best and having the best – as each individual defines "the best." For some, "best" is the place where they could participate in Greek life and live out a version of the movie *Animal House*. For others, it was about the place that would provide them a great pre-med experience so that they could become a doctor. And for still others, it was the opportunity to be able to play sports.

Devin was not going to play sports at UT-Austin, but being a Longhorns fan excited him. Talikha wanted to get out of state and to a highly ranked school that would position her for her still-undefined future – and where she could have ready access to faculty, advisors, clubs, and job opportunities. And Ujana wanted a great singing experience with a solid early childhood program. People who experience this Job feel like they have put in the work and earned the opportunity to have the "best for them" in their pursuit of being "the best."

Figure 3.1 Help me get into my best school.

- So I can have the classic "college experience"
- So I can live in a brick-and-mortar college
- So I can belong to a place with prestige/a great reputation
- So I can reinvent myself and meet new people
- When I need to take the next logical step

If you are experiencing this Job, it's also likely that you are asking a version of "Who am I?" – a refrain much of society associates with the exploratory nature of the stereotypical four-year college experience. There's a lot of energy animating this question. And if you have this Job, like those we interviewed, you are probably feeling some mixture of excitement and nervous energy around the aspirational nature of this Job (Figure 3.1).

Most of the students who experienced this Job in our research were the "traditional" college students who wanted the full "college experience" they had been led – or taught – to expect, be that from their siblings, parents, friends, teachers, counselors, or Hollywood. Ninety-one percent of the students who experienced this Job in our interviews were 18- to 25-years-old; 85% attended college full-time; and the vast majority – 79% – were from middle-class households. Seventy-two percent said they had no prior work experience, which mirrors the fact that far fewer teenagers – 20% – hold a job today compared to 1990, when nearly 40% did.[5]

But you don't have to be a "traditional" college-aged student to experience this Job – nor do you have to be getting your bachelor's degree.

One of the coauthors of this book, Michael, experienced this Job at least twice in his life. The first time was when he went to college. A second time was when he went to business school. After graduating college, Michael worked in a two-year job. Everyone before him in that position had gone to law school after the two years, but Michael was not sure that was what he wanted. In his second year working, he applied to business schools and law schools around the country with the intention of doing a joint JD-MBA degree. He was accepted to several law and business programs at the same university. But at Harvard he only got into the business school, not the law school. When he took his parents to see the Harvard Business School campus, his parents marveled with him at its beauty, facilities, and access to unbelievable learning opportunities and connections. It felt like the "best" place he could be. His Dad told him as much. Sure enough, the decision was effectively sealed. A couple weeks later, Michael chose to attend the Harvard Business School and figured he would reapply to the Law School once he was enrolled. After one week as a first-year student, however, he decided to forget about law school. He admitted to himself that he really did not want to be a lawyer. And he was having a lot of fun in business school.

HOW TO BE SUCCESSFUL WHEN YOU HAVE THIS JOB ARISE IN YOUR LIFE

Although the vast majority of students that we interviewed who experienced this Job were satisfied with their choice, this was not always the case. Here's how to avoid the risks associated with this Job and come out a winner.

Step 1: Know Thyself

First, if the college-choosing decision is stressing you out, relax.

As we detailed in the previous chapter, you will get into a school. If your goal is to get into a highly selective school, the odds are even better today than a generation ago that you will get into one. And if you go to a nonselective school, work hard, and build a strong network – at school or afterward – you can do more than just fine. You can become a leader in any field.[6]

You don't want to be like Kolby, whom we profiled in the previous chapter, and bank your sense of self-worth on this one decision.

And you don't want to get caught in the pressure that some students in places like Lexington, Massachusetts; Palo Alto, California; or Bethesda, Maryland, feel. Those communities have attracted national notoriety for a high-stress atmosphere around getting into college that has contributed to some students taking their own lives. In Palo Alto, five students committed suicide in a nine-month span between May 2009 and January 2010. Three more took their lives between October 2014 and April 2015.[7] According to the New York Times, in a 2015 survey, "95% of Lexington High School students reported being heavily stressed over their classes and 15% said they had considered killing themselves in the last year."[8] Walt Whitman High School, from which Michael is a graduate, in Bethesda, has an entire book written about the pressure its students feel, titled *The Overachievers: The Secret Lives of Driven Kids* by Alexandra Robbins.[9]

So take a deep breath. And then several more. Remember: Life is a journey, not a destination. There are many pathways you can take.

Second, more important than stressing out about whether you will get into a good school is figuring out what's the right fit for you.

Not what others think is best. Not what the rankings say is best. What is best *for you*. Right now.

One student, who had this Job, Grace, made a choice based on what she wanted others to think about her, not what was best for her regardless of what others thought.

Grace received a full-tuition scholarship her senior year of high school to play ice hockey at an out-of-state public school with a nationally ranked ice hockey program. The flagship public university in her state, which had a sterling ranking and national reputation for academics, as well as a really strong ice hockey team, also offered her a chance to play ice hockey. And it accepted her into its honors college.

As Grace considered her options, she realized she did not want to play hockey – and go to school. She wanted to go to school – and play hockey. With an emphasis on being a student above being an athlete, she made her choice. Staying in-state and attending the nationally ranked flagship school so she could tell others that she was in the honors college felt really good. Being able to say she would play hockey there felt like icing on the cake. To her parents, it felt like a lot of pressure.

Once college started, Grace never let her friends in the honors college know that she was an ice hockey player, and she never talked about the honors college with her ice hockey teammates. She kept her academic and athletic lives separate. Soon, the workloads from each mounted. The task of balancing them became too much. The pressure cascaded around her, on top of which she did not like her classes at all. With no plan B, she dropped out after her freshman year.

This story illustrates a lurking danger in this Job. If you have unrealistic expectations or you are doing things because of what you want others to think of you, you might make a decision that is inconsistent with what "best" is for you.

More generally, this can be a dangerous Job because you often have a vague sense of your future. You're trying to get into the "best for you" without a clear sense of what will happen next. That means you probably don't know what you are optimizing for.

It can be hard to make a smart decision with so many unknowns. All too often in life we procrastinate by solving for the unknowns last because it just feels easier. But you can reverse the script.

Before making some choices about where to apply, turn some of the unknowns into knowns and clarify your vision.

Here are some ideas to get you started:

- **Focus on your strengths.** Take Gallup's Strengths-Finder assessment, which you can access by buying the *StrengthsFinders 2.0* book on Amazon, to gain valuable insight into your strengths, a realistic picture of where you excel, and the opportunity to focus by allowing you to pick a program that will build on those strengths.

- **Think about your passions.** Consider not what you think you need to do to impress someone in a college admissions office but what truly excites you. Life's too short to be spending most of it in things you don't like doing. To help you, write down every time you feel excited and happy each day and notice what brings you those feelings of excitement. Contrast that with when you're feeling bored, stressed, or disengaged. Then think about how you can get more of the positive things in school – whether that's a particular extracurricular activity or just the ability to try lots of new things and learn about who you are.

- **Leverage a variation of a tool from one of the most popular books of all time, *What Color Is Your Parachute?* by Richard N. Bolles.** Make a "seven-petal diagram" (Figure 3.2) that reflects the different

Figure 3.2 The petals on your college flower.

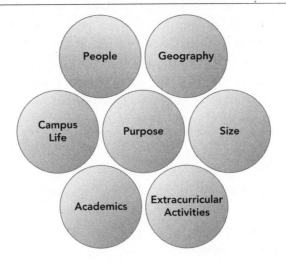

aspects you value, using the language of college.[10] Focus on your desires around the people at a school (such things as the students, faculty, and staff), geography (near or far; urban, rural, suburban, or online), size (small, medium, big), campus life (safety, parties, support services, residential, or commuter), academics (departments, classes, teaching, times of classes), extracurricular activities, and what best matches your purpose in going. **Notice that we don't have a petal for price.** That's intentional. At this stage, don't worry too much about price. You're trying to figure out what experience is best for you – not the specific college yet. The price tag will enter the equation later and force you to make tradeoffs. Having a clear idea of what you want and do not want will help you make those tradeoffs.

Exploring each of these petals will likely take some serious thought. And that's the point. It will also start to prepare you for when you actually enroll in college so you're ready to seize the experience and engage fully. You may also not have strong preferences in certain of the areas. That's OK, too. Whether a school was small, medium, or big was not that important to Devin, for example.

To get started, think about what you value or detest along a variety of metrics, including:

Geography

- Close vs. far away
- Urban vs. suburban vs. rural

Size

- Small vs. medium vs. large
- Small college experiences nestled inside of a large campus vs. a large community

Extracurricular Activities

- Many opportunities to participate in athletics vs. limited opportunities
- Vibrant extracurricular activities vs. focus on academics
- Career-related activities vs. hobbies
- Performance arts vs. visual arts
- Competitive activities vs. open/non-competitive ones

Academics

- Focus on academics vs. vibrant extracurricular activities
- Depth vs. breadth of offerings
- Choice in courses vs. prescribed course sequences
- Large lectures vs. small seminars
- Liberal arts focus vs. career technical focus

Campus Life

- Greek life vs. no Greek life
- Commuter school vs. residential experience
- On-campus dining culture vs. off-campus dining culture

- Public vs. private
- Strong athletic teams vs. weak ones

People

- Diverse array of students vs. students similar to you
- Students from around the world vs. students from nearby
- Students with diverse interests vs. students with narrow, focused interests
- Emphasis on research faculty vs. faculty focused on teaching
- Access to structured supports (mentors, counselors, administration) vs. more independence

Purpose

- Strong spiritual/religious focus vs. little spiritual/religious focus
- Focus on community vs. focus on developing the individual

We've framed these as tradeoffs on purpose to try and force you to think about what your priorities are. You might not have opinions on all or any of these particular dimensions. There may be specific elements of some of these that are most important or an element important to you that is not listed here. You may not know what you value until you visit schools and start to see what you gravitate toward. If you visit a small school in a city and like it, test whether it's the city campus that you like or the fact that the school is small by visiting a large school in a city.

But make sure you do not choose a school in opposition to what you value. As you work through your seven petals, defining what is a nonstarter might matter more than defining what you do value because you just might not know what you really want at this point in your life. If a big school would be a terrible fit, for example, then it is important to be honest about that with yourself, but it is OK to be unsure of what you do want. College can be a great place to explore.

Third, before you've done the hard work of figuring out what is right for you, throw out all the rankings lists. Even after you have done the hard work of figuring out what you want, you should still probably throw out the rankings lists. The common rankings of college – from *U.S. News & World Report* to *Princeton Review* – do not represent what is best for you. According to research from a variety of sources, including researchers from Stanford, most rankings don't even represent what college is best in general, let alone what the right fit for you is.[11]

In *Where You Go Is Not Who You Will Be,* Jeffrey Brenzel, the former dean of admissions at Yale, laments how students "jettison carefully constructed lists of colleges that might be right for them in favor of lists with a familiar cast of schools ... 'that always seem to correlate with the rankings in *U.S. News....* The simplicity and clarity that ranking systems seem to offer are not only misleading, but can also be harmful.... Rankings tend to ignore the very criteria that may be most important to an applicant, such as specific academic offerings, intellectual and social climate, ease of access to faculty, international opportunities and placement rates for careers or for graduate and professional school.'"[12]

Former Stanford Provost and Secretary of State Condoleezza Rice agrees. Bruni summarized her thoughts: "[Rankings] unnecessarily shrink the pool of schools that kids consider … and give short shrift to the multitude and diversity of them, and they imply that certain schools are better for everyone, when they may only be better for particular students with particular dispositions."[13]

Instead, to thy own self be true. Find a college that is the best fit for you.

Step 2: Identify Matches

Once you have your criteria in place, spend time finding schools that are right for you. Here's where various guides, college databases, software tools like Naviance, and some rankings can help. The *Fiske Guide to Colleges*, for example, has a plethora of information on hundreds of colleges so you can filter and see which schools might fit your interests. *The College Finder* and *College Match* focus on which types of schools might be good fits for you. *Princeton Review*'s guide allows you to filter based on a variety of categories, from "great schools for agriculture majors" to schools with the "most politically active students." *Barron's Profiles of American Colleges* is an online search engine allowing you to match your academic plans with admissions criteria to find a desirable school, as well as advice on everything from how to get the most out of a campus visit to profiles of over 1650 schools categorized by state. The *Washington Monthly*'s rankings can help you figure out the best bang for the buck, the best colleges for adult learners, and the best schools for social mobility.

Talk to your guidance or college counselor about what schools might fit your criteria. Do research on the Internet. And if you can, visit schools so you can test your assumptions around what is best for you and which schools truly match that criteria.

If you know that price may be a factor in where you go, use the rankings and guides, counselors, and other mentors in your life to broaden your list of options that align with your criteria. Spend time examining in-state options; places that offer financial aid based on need, not merit; and schools that may be less expensive.

Do not add schools to your list that you wouldn't be excited to attend or just because someone in your life – your parent, a sibling, a friend, or a counselor – thinks it is a "great school." It's not worth the application fee. If you're wondering whether you should add a certain safety school to your list, consider if it meets your criteria and you would enroll enthusiastically. Adding a college just because you feel like you should when you wouldn't enjoy going to it could be a costly mistake because it pushes you into the Help Me Do What's Expected of Me Job, which we discuss in the next chapter.

Despite the narrative you've bought into that school is the next logical step, you don't have to go to school right away. There are other options, such as taking a gap year. For example, one student we talked to, Delilah, who was the first in her family to go to college, applied to just one school that had a terrific cheerleading team when she graduated high school. Unfortunately because it was an out-of-state school, she wasn't able to afford it. She decided to work at the nearby Burger King to make some money for groceries and a car while she researched local schools. Her mom respected her decision, but **made sure Delilah had a plan.**

This appears to be vital. If you take a gap year, particularly if it's for financial or family reasons, make sure you have a plan. That plan can be to learn more about you. Just be sure you have a defined time horizon over which you will execute that plan. You want to use this period in your life to step it up into the next phase of your life (more on this in Chapter 6), not drift aimlessly.

At her mom's request, Delilah studied her old high school materials a couple hours a week on her own while she worked and researched her options so that she wouldn't "lose touch with that school aspect," she said. She fell in love with a nearby school that had a competitive cheerleading team. Delilah applied, was accepted, enrolled, and loved the experience.

The bottom line? You do you and stick to it.

Step 3: Check and Choose

Once you have created your list for where you want to apply, check that the choices make sense. Spend time getting to know them on the Internet. Visit the schools when you can. And either before or after you've been accepted, take a page from Talikha and Ujana. Talk to current students and alumni of the school to figure out what it is really like and get a flavor of whether a school is for you – or, at minimum, if something about the school is a nonstarter for you.

To repeat – don't fall into the trap of choosing a school just because everyone around you says it's great. You should feel excited about it, and it should meet your criteria, not someone else's. You're the one who will be going to classes and putting in the work over the next few years, not someone else. You should be enthusiastic and committed.

Finally, once you've fulfilled this Job – assuming you get into one of your "best" schools and, after factoring in price, you decide to go – prepare for what comes next.

As Bruni describes, too few students today think about what comes after they enroll. You don't want to be paralyzed once you're accepted – "frozen" and "adrift." One of Bruni's students at Princeton described arriving on campus and experiencing a letdown, saying, "I kind of felt like I put so much energy into getting in the first place that once I got in, I didn't know what to do."[14]

It's true that you can remain in variations of the Help Me Get into My Best School Job for some time – "Help me get into the 'best' club on campus," "Help me get my best leadership position in an extracurricular activity," "Help me get my best job when I graduate." Some professors speculate that the reason Ivy League graduates aim for jobs on Wall Street is because the process of getting "the best" job and beating out others is familiar.[15]

But at some point – and perhaps as soon as you enroll or maybe even just before – you are likely to come off the "Help me get into my best" treadmill. Rather than the focus being on "getting in," you will think about what you want from an experience. What do you want to learn, what doors do you want to have opened, what is driving you intrinsically as opposed to extrinsically? Remember: Life is a journey, not a destination.

When that pivot happens in your life – and as your circumstances shift, that pivot will almost certainly happen – you want to be ready. If you fit squarely into this Job right now in your life, the rest of Part II will prepare you for your lifelong learning journey when those times come. Because although this Job, entrenched as it is in the popular narrative, may be the most familiar one for why students go to college, you have a whole lifetime of learning where you'll use education to help you make progress.

WHAT TO DO IF YOU ARE A PARENT OF A CHILD WITH THIS JOB

If you are the parent of a child or a friend of someone who has this Job, we have six pieces of advice.

1. **If you live in a high-pressure environment or you see your child is stressed about the college admissions process, help her relax.** Take the pressure off – through the stories and stats we, and others, provide – and certainly don't add to the pressure. That doesn't mean just *telling* your child to relax, but *showing* through your actions and words that relaxing is not only OK, it's a good idea. Support your child – directly and by helping him get access to the external support he might need. And make sure he knows your love is unconditional.

2. **Throw out the rankings lists.** We already said why the rankings won't help and could hurt. A rankings list isn't just a poor way to figure out the right fit for your child, it could also add to the stress of the college admissions process. See our advice in point number one.

3. **Help your child define what is important and what is a nonstarter – for her, not you.** Your child will be going to school, not you. Remember that. By the same token, if you see your child has unrealistic expectations, help guide her toward a more realistic picture of what is best for her. Make the tradeoffs in her decisions clear.

   If you do not feel capable of helping your child with the decision – maybe you did not go to college, for example, or your child has tuned you out – helping your child find a trusted mentor, having her talk to one of your friends, or creating a relationship with an advisor in or outside of school could be a way to help still. Several of the students we talked to whose parents had not gone to college found their "best school" through a mentor.

   Lawrence, for example, who had served in the Marines after high school and whose story we told earlier in this chapter, struck up a friendship by chance with a professor at Georgia Tech, who guided him through the college application process and suggested strong alternatives to Georgia Tech. Once Lawrence was in college, he continued to meet his mentor every week.

   Kurt, another student who was the first in his family to go to college, worked as a guidance counselor's assistant during his senior year of high school. As a result, his guidance counselor offered him extra help as he navigated the college application process.

4. **Help broaden the choices that your child has so she can find the right match for what is best for her.** You might take her to visit a range of schools that

have lots of different features and characteristics. See what she gravitates to and away from in the set of schools and see what is consistent. This would help you understand what dimensions she seems to be valuing and which are nonstarters. You may be able to see things about your child that she cannot see about herself. Then you could show her more schools along the dimensions she seems to be valuing to help her have choices and be accepted to a school that matches what she truly wants.

5. **Most important, if your child does not get into the school she wants to go to, do not force her to go to a school about which she is not excited.** Do not have her apply to schools in the first place that violate her nonstarters or the criteria she values – say, because you want to live your life or your own hopes and dreams through your child, or because you're worried about price. If you're worried about price, then find other colleges that are both affordable and exciting to her. If she's not enthusiastic about her college options, then help her find a gap-year experience where she can learn about herself, a job, a fifth-year of high school at a prep school for athletics, or something else.

   If your child goes this route, be like Delilah's mom. Support her, but also make sure your child has a plan that is time-bound to figure things out. In the absence of guardrails, it could become easy for a gap year in a low-wage job with limited pathways toward fulfilling opportunities, for example, to stretch on without end.

Pushing your child into something she does not want and is doing to fulfill your expectations will move her into the Help Me Do What's Expected of Me Job we unearthed in our research, which is not ideal. We turn to that Job in the next chapter. But know that avoiding this outcome might even mean seeing if you and your child can find a creative solution to afford the high price tag of your child's dream institution. The alternative – pushing her into the Help Me Do What's Expected of Me Job – is a bad idea.

6. **Prepare your child to pivot Jobs.** Once she's in, it's likely she will move to a new Job, but maybe even encourage and help her in that shift. Life isn't just about climbing a linear ladder and getting into things. It's about what you do once you're into something. And it's ideally about doing things about which you are genuinely passionate so you can lead a purposeful, happy and fulfilling life. Getting into your child's best school can certainly advance that cause, but it's unlikely to be the end of the story. That means allowing her to cultivate her interests, pursue her passions, and do things about which she is intrinsically excited. Help her build self-awareness around those passions, likes, dislikes, and strengths, so that she can handle the other struggles she will inevitably have in life and make wise decisions.

WHAT NOT TO DO

WHAT TO DO

Choosing College: How to Make Better Learning Decisions

Chapter 4

Help Me Do What's Expected of Me

What happens if you don't get into one of your dream schools and you're unexcited by your remaining schooling options?

GOING FOR OTHERS

If you still plan to go to school because you feel like you're supposed to satisfy others' expectations of you – like those of your parents, spouse, friends, guidance counselor, teacher, mentor, employer, or community – then there is a good chance you are having school help you do what's expected of you.

Students experience this Job when:

- They need to satisfy or obey people in their life.

- They need to take the next logical step.

- They don't have or can't see any other options besides school.

They enroll so:

- They can check the box with a degree.

- They have a safety net and something to fall back on just in case things go sideways in their life.

People who experienced this Job often immediately recognized it in themselves.

They told us about the clergy member at their church or synagogue who told them they should go to school. Or how their parents couldn't imagine them not going. They recounted the pressure they felt to go along, even though they weren't personally that excited about enrolling.

This Job is sometimes the other side of the coin for people who don't get into their dream school – *but not always.* Often, it just felt like going to school was the next step in their lives because that's what people expected them to do. They never had a dream school. They felt indifferent about school, and they weren't sure why they were going.

Many students who had this Job were dissatisfied with their college experience. That's in direct contrast to the majority of those who went to school to help them get into their best school. Yet some told us that, in retrospect, they appreciated the push to go even though college wasn't great.

Despite those retrospective feelings of gratitude, which are real and important, the advice we offer for those experiencing this Job is designed to help you avoid the worst-case scenario and help you enjoy whatever is next in your life, not just go through the motions. We seek to help you use this step in your life as a springboard to building passion and finding fulfillment.

But first, to help you recognize whether this Job describes where you are, here are three stories of students who experienced the Help Me Do What's Expected of Me Job.

MADDY'S STORY

Maddy received a lot of mail from colleges while in high school. Most of it went into the recycling bin. But she kept a few pamphlets around. Soon she started visiting some of those campuses to figure out where she should apply.

She traveled to several schools and started to get a sense for what she wanted. As a high school athlete – she played softball, volleyball, and was a cheerleader – having a full college experience with a football team to root for and clubs to participate in while living in a true college town was important. And although she had no intention of coming back home all that often during college, being within a day's drive of home so she could get back just in case seemed important, too.

After visits to several colleges, her state's flagship university felt right for her. It was 45 minutes from home, located in a classic college town, and had a lively campus with great sports teams. She got excited thinking about going to school there. She was a classic case of seeking to get into her best school.

Her family and friends were sure she would get in, but just in case, Maddy decided to apply to five colleges in total – three public universities in state and two out-of-state public universities. She wanted some options in case she did not get in to her dream school.

As acceptance decisions started arriving, Maddy heard from the other four schools first. She got into every single one, but did not think much of it. She was waiting to hear from her state's flagship university.

When at last she did, the news was mixed. She had been accepted, but for the following spring semester – meaning she would not be allowed to enroll in the fall.

She was heartbroken, and she felt embarrassed. Many of Maddy's friends had received full scholarships to attend the state flagship university, and here she was not even able to attend. Everyone was gearing up to go away – her best friends, everyone – and, as she said, "I didn't want to be just sitting there. It was like, 'Oh my gosh, everyone's going to judge me'. … I was really excited about college and getting started also."

Maddy began looking at her other options. She ruled out one out-of-state school because it was too expensive. She nixed one of the in-state schools because it was her safety school. It was down to two options – an out-of-state school where her two best friends were going and an in-state school where her boyfriend attended, but which did not have much of a campus life.

Truth be told, she was not excited about either option. She did not want to attend school with her best friends.

She wanted to use college as an opportunity to redefine her potential, and she knew she would always have them as best friends, she said. The in-state school, however, felt like the opposite of the classic college experience to her. It did not have a football team and was not in a college town.

She spent a week mulling over the two schools with her parents and friends. She felt like her parents would be happiest if she attended in-state because it would be less expensive. Additionally, her brother had gone to college there and, before she was born, her dad had taught there. She knew her boyfriend was there, too, but she tried not to think about him as she made the decision. Still, she did not feel excited about attending the in-state college. She was torn.

A couple nights later, she was talking about the decision with her friends when they pointed out that she could go to the in-state institution for a semester or a year, and if she really hated it, she could just transfer. That would be far less risky and expensive than going to the out-of-state college that she did not really want to attend. That reassurance, that "I could go here, and if it's as bad as people say and I hate it, I can always go somewhere else," just gave Maddy the confidence that she should start her college experience that fall when "everyone" else did, in-state about 15 minutes away from her home, and with the mindset that she could always transfer.

TRISHA'S STORY

Trisha attended two different private Christian high schools in Ohio. She had always assumed she would go to college after graduating. "It was pretty much instilled in both school settings that you were going to go to college. And you were kind of the oddball of the group if you decided not to go. I always thought that you go through grade school, you go through junior high, you go through high school, and then you go to college. It was never an option in my brain that I wouldn't," she said. Both of her parents were supportive as well.

Throughout her schooling experience, she had a sense that women could only grow up to do one of three careers: be a teacher, go into the ministry, or become a secretary. Her first school had also only talked about one Christian school in Indiana that she could go to. She did not know there were other options.

During her senior year, she and others in her church youth group sat down with her church pastor, and he opened their eyes to lots of other Christian college options. He told them about each school's style of teaching, their Biblical stance, and more.

Seeing the college process as something you just did next, Trisha asked her pastor where he thought she would do best. He knew she preferred smaller settings, and so he advised her to attend a particular Christian school in Tennessee. Trisha never visited the school. She just applied because her pastor said it would be a good fit. She was accepted, and she enrolled.

GREG'S STORY

The son of illegal immigrants who had spent much of their lives toiling in manual jobs, Greg heard often about the importance of education. After high school, he earned an associate degree from the local university. His parents footed the entire tuition bill. He then began working as an EMT and applied a few times to a nearby university to receive a bachelor's degree in emergency management.

For a variety of reasons, Greg's plans to continue his education kept stalling, but he was not heartbroken by the setbacks and the lack of a bachelor's degree. Instead, he was experiencing a lot of momentum in his career. After three years as an EMT, he got a job as a medical specialist in a plasma donation clinic and moved quickly up to be the medical operations supervisor. Paraphrasing novelist Grant Allen, Greg said, "I never let my education get in the way of my success. The best lessons in life come from experience, not from a teacher." Life continued to teach him this lesson.

Although he was considering trying to go back to school to get a bachelor's in emergency management, doing so did not make much sense from his perspective. He was moving up the ranks in his company, and the center where he worked was one of the top-performing clinics in both the state and nation. He was receiving a lot of positive feedback, and he felt like he did not necessarily need more education to continue to move upward.

Then his company made him aware of a new opportunity. It had entered into a partnership with a new online program that offered a competency-based degree – meaning that you made progress toward the degree as you demonstrated mastery of the program's core learning objectives, not based on time. That meant you could move as slow or fast as you could through the program to get your bachelor's degree. And his company would pay for the whole education.

Greg did not think much of the offer until he saw one of his colleagues try it and get her associate degree in just six months. He decided to apply and was accepted. He enrolled a month later. Although it was not a convenient time for him to be working and enrolled in an online university – he was getting married just a few months later – he figured having his bachelor's might give him a slight leg up as he continued to move up the corporate ladder, even as the lack of it had not hurt him to this point. He admitted that the program was not relevant to his job, and he also wondered aloud about his family members who did have bachelor's degrees and yet were making less money than he was. But ultimately, he said, he knew that having his bachelor's would make his parents proud – and that was motivation enough to get started, especially given his company was paying all the tuition.

UNDERSTANDING THE HELP ME DO WHAT'S EXPECTED OF ME JOB

If you are experiencing this Job, then you are considering schools for an extrinsic reason – to do what is expected of you. That expectation can be from a variety of sources – a parent, family member, mentor, school, peers, employer, or the broader community and society. The line between this Job and the Help Me Get into My Best School Job is thin, but even as there are some similarities, there are also important distinctions.

Maddy felt like she could not be the only one of her friends and classmates staying home in the fall. Trisha's pastor told her where to go. Greg felt he should enroll because of his parents and because his employer helped make the decision a "might as well do it" – even though the online program was not relevant for his work.

Given these dynamics, students experiencing this Job are apathetic about their choice. They lack the excitement that students in the Help Me Get into My Best School Job have typically. Every Job to Be Done has energy – the effort one puts in to make a decision. This Job had by far the lowest energy of any of the Jobs we discovered. Students' choices were passive.

- **You probably see no choice for what's next in your life besides education if you have this Job.** As in the Help Me Get into My Best School Job, there's a good chance your current reality is ending – perhaps you're graduating from high school – and so you have to do something else.

- **College feels like the next logical step.** Greg is an exception here, as he was not forced to attend (it's important to note that not every story perfectly matches each Job description), but Maddy's and Trisha's stories both fit this pattern.

- **If you are in this Job, you are likely going primarily because someone else either explicitly or implicitly demanded you do so.** As opposed to those experiencing the Help Me Get into My Best School Job, students with this Job have little passion about where they are going and often a lot of ambivalence, which describes Maddy's, Trisha's, and Greg's situations. The students often see little choice or autonomy in the matter.

- **Students sometimes fall into this Job if they do not get into or are not allowed to attend their top choice schools for some reason, such as financial or geographical.** In other words, they are in the Help Me Get into My Best School Job, but then move into this Job. Maddy was in this boat. She didn't get into her dream school when she felt she should, and she didn't feel like she could wait to go.

- **Students sometimes feel that enrollment is simply a box to check.** Maddy, like many who have this Job, saw enrollment as an expectation. Greg felt the same way. The degree was a box to check and then move on.

Many students who experience this Job comfort themselves with the idea that a college degree will provide them with a safety net or foundation for the rest of their lives (see Figure 4.1).

Although demographics – features like your race, your age, whether you are the first in your family to attend college, and how many children you have – don't tell us what Job to Be Done you are in because they don't tell us

Figure 4.1 Help me do what's expected of me.

- When I need to satisfy/obey people in my life
  - Some had a "dream school" but failed to get in
- So I can check the box
- When I don't have/can't see any other options
- When I need to take the next logical step
- So I have a safety net/something to fall back on

anything about what you are trying to accomplish in your specific circumstance, they can provide more context of how to help individuals be successful when they have a certain Job. We found two different *personas* – meaning representations of a group of individuals based on their demographics – in this Job.

The first persona, which made up the majority of our sample, was the "traditional" 18- to 25-year-old college student. Eighty-four percent of people in our research who experienced this Job fell into that age bracket, and 72% said they had no prior work experience. The storyline generally closely mirrored Maddy's. And it could happen to all sorts of students. Florence, for example, had her heart set on going to a university in New York City with her best friend. She got in, but her dad told her that they could not afford the school – and the more affordable state flagship university she got into was ranked higher anyway. She enrolled begrudgingly at the state university in the south far from New York City.

The second persona resembles Greg more closely. It's made up of working adults who feel that their employer or family expects them to go back to college even though there is not an obvious or compelling reason to attend outside of circumstances making it easy to enroll – such as their employer will foot the bill.

HOW TO BE SUCCESSFUL WHEN YOU HAVE THIS JOB ARISE IN YOUR LIFE

Fifty-four percent of those who experienced this Job were dissatisfied with their schooling experience. A whopping 74% ended up transferring or dropping out.

Trisha fell into this category. When she showed up on campus on day one, it was the first time she had been out of Ohio. She felt immediately homesick. She did fine in her courses, but her heart was not in it. She did not want to leave the dorm. She did not meet that many people at the school.

Toward the end of her first semester, circumstances back home worsened. Trisha's parents could no longer afford the college's tuition bill. Given she was homesick and not enjoying the college experience, Trisha decided it was time to leave rather than seek out loans or try to work to continue to attend.

Some who were dissatisfied did see a silver lining. Although they may not have enjoyed their college experience, years later they were glad that they had gone along with what their parents or community expected of them. They felt like it had been worth it. One person we talked to who experienced this Job said she would never have gone to college had her parents not demanded she do so. She didn't enjoy the experience or her major, and she transferred schools before graduating in five years. But 20 years later, she was glad she had gone.

That's important perspective. If you are in this Job, we encourage you to try to feel gratitude that you have the opportunity to go to college now, which can create a lot of value in your life. Many do not have this opportunity and would do just about anything to be in your shoes. Of course, it's not easy to just "feel thankful." One way you can cultivate those feelings of gratitude is by keeping a gratitude journal, in which you simply jot down a few things for which you are grateful each day. The benefits of doing so can extend from increasing your positivity to helping you sleep better.[1]

With that said, our advice is not just to try to feel gratitude. Yes, it's true that you can get through life by doing things that are "good for you" but that you don't enjoy. Getting a college degree because your parents insisted you do so can fall into this camp. But you should demand more in your life. By understanding the Job you're experiencing, you can take hold of your circumstances and move quickly into a new Job in which you're able to do something for intrinsic reasons and derive value. Doing so will increase your odds of success and help you minimize risk. Our research revealed three pathways that allowed students to reframe their experience and switch Jobs.

Step 1: Know Thyself

If you were in the Help Me Get into My Best School Job, but didn't get into any of your dream schools and you've moved into this Job, acknowledge it. Your circumstances have changed, which means how you approach choosing school should change, too.

If you were never excited about going to college but you felt like you had to, or if your employer has thrown this opportunity in front of you, but you can't figure out why you should go other than that it's easy, recognize that, too.

Knowing this doesn't mean you won't go to school but acknowledging the feeling of being on a moving walkway without an off-ramp because of others' expectations is important.

Be mindful that committing mentally and financially to something long-term could be difficult because your heart isn't in it. There's a reason why 74% of students with this Job transfer or drop out.

Step 2: Identify Matches

If you read this book and you identify with the Help Me Get into My Best School Job, then don't add safety schools to your college applications for their own sake unless you would be excited to attend them. This will help you avoid falling into this Job.

If you are already in this pathway, one option is to swallow your pride about what other people expect you to do, avoid wasting the money, and opt out of this Job. Recognize where you are and fight to take a gap year – not to travel aimlessly around Europe but to learn about yourself and build a passion through a series of short jobs, internships, volunteer projects, apprenticeships, bootcamps, online courses, temp agencies, and the like.

One person, Ed Shartar, we talked to did just this. "I was putting a lot of pressure on myself to figure out at 18 what I should be doing for the rest of my life, and I was clueless," he said. "It dawned on me that I was going to college not because it was what I wanted, but because it was expected of me. I decided that was a lousy reason.... At that point, I realized I needed to take time off and get my act together." Ed went to Israel instead and worked on a kibbutz, which was a life-altering experience. At the end of a year he had the opportunity to stay in Israel, but he had developed a clear sense of what he wanted college to do for him and chose to attend. As he told us, "The operative word is *chose*. The big difference from before is that previously I was [going to college] because it was expected of me, so I basically delegated the decision to those around me. Now, it was completely my decision. . . . I entered college with a greater seriousness and a goal to take full advantage of what college had to offer academically."

Despite the potential benefits of a gap year, there is reason to be cautious. Some research suggests that low-income students who take time off may struggle to get back into a college track for a variety of reasons. If you take time off, make sure you spend it learning more and learning about yourself. That might mean you find a mentor who helps you line up a series of paid jobs in unfamiliar fields. It could mean you take a job in a field where there are opportunities for advancement long-term. If you're curious which fields fall into that description, we recommend checking out resources like the report "When Is a Job Just a Job – And When Can It Launch a Career?"[2] Even though you will likely need more education to qualify for one of those jobs with advancement opportunities, you can learn whether you even like the field. We also recommend searching sites like the Gap Year Association (https://www.gapyearassociation.org), which can help you unearth paid opportunities, gap year programs like Global Citizen Year that offer financial aid based on need, or programs that offer some college credit even as you work.

If you're a working adult, defer the benefit being offered and keep working. There will be many more educational opportunities as you progress in your career.

With all that said, opting out of this Job or not applying to backup schools can be really hard. You have to overcome a lot of social pressure pushing you to attend and a lot of conventional wisdom about what you should do next.

Step 3: Check and Choose

If you do choose to attend school, tighten your time horizon.

What we mean is that when you enroll, commit mentally to a fraction of the experience, not the entirety of it. Think about your enrollment as lasting only for a semester or a year. During that time period, reevaluate what you are doing. Tightening your time horizon will force you to think about choices – should you transfer, drop out, take time off, or continue to attend, for example – which forces you back in the position of "shopping" with the chance to change the Job you are experiencing. When students took this advice, we saw three pathways out of the Help Me Do What's Expected of Me Job.

Pathway 1: Change to the Help Me Get into My Best School Job

Maddy entered college with low expectations, under the assumption that she could transfer, which made her choice safe and low-risk. It also meant she was shopping and back in the Help Me Get into My Best School Job from day one. Once on campus, she realized that the school she was attending had a lot to offer academically in ways that would not have been true at the state's flagship school. Her feelings shifted, and she embraced the experience. Her "best" school turned out not to be a school she would have to transfer to, but where she was.

Maddy also chose a school that was low-risk and from which it would be easy to transfer because it was in state. This was smart, and it offers one lesson.

If you are experiencing this Job and you will attend school, choose one that is as low-risk and low-stakes as possible. That means it should be as low-cost and convenient as possible. It should allow you to transfer the credits that you earn to other colleges. And remember, if it feels strange to have this mindset as you pick a school, if you build a strong network and work hard at nearly any college, you can be successful in life.

After a semester, Florence similarly realized that the in-state school she was attending was a top school with great offerings that could get her ahead in her dream to be a doctor. If she played her cards right, she could attend medical school in New York City and still live out that dream.

If you find yourself like Maddy and Florence – back in the Help Me Get into My Best School Job – put everything into the process of finding that right fit during the semester or year. Learn to appreciate your current school and what it offers or transfer somewhere that will be the best fit for you.

Pathway 2: Change to the Help Me Step It Up Job

Bob, one of the coauthors of this book, had an experience in college that illustrates another possible pathway out of this Job. When Bob did not get into his dream school years ago and experienced the Help Me Do What's Expected of Me Job, he enrolled at the nearby regional university that was in state.

Like Maddy and Florence, Bob tightened his time horizon. But he moved into a different Job – Help Me Step It Up. We explore this Job in Chapter 5. But in short, students experience this Job when they don't recognize themselves in some part of their life – they want to get away from a paid job, role, or habit – and are ready to step it up and do better.

What you need to know for now is that Bob decided to search for outside work while he was enrolled in college to help him step it up. He found a part-time job a couple hours away from campus and soon realized that he wanted to spend all of his time working. He had found a passion. To get hired full-time, however, his boss said he had to finish his degree – so Bob did.

If you fall into this Job, you can give yourself 6–12 months to find a paid job, career, or something else you really want to do and about which you are passionate. Then dig in to build that passion and take the necessary steps to enable you to do it full-time. You can do that while you're enrolled in college, like Bob, or, if you opt out of this Job, you can do it instead of going to school.

Pathway 3: Change to the Help Me Get Away Job

Another story illustrates a third pathway out of this Job after you have tightened your time horizon.

A student named Juan did not know why he was in college.[3] He enrolled because the No Excuses charter school – a public chartered school that does not accept any excuses for the achievement gap between poor minorities and their more affluent, white counterparts – he had gone to said he had to attend college and had helped him every step of the way with his application and enrollment.

But with his uncertainty about why he was enrolled and lack of purpose, when the experience created a significant financial toll on his family, Juan decided to take action and drop out to move to a new stage of his life. He in essence moved to the Help Me Get Away Job – a Job that we explore in the next chapter, in which students are looking to get away from a current job, break a current habit, or leave home and their family, town, or a particular relationship – to escape college. Although to many this might sound irresponsible because dropping out of college is seen as a "bad" outcome, it was actually a very responsible decision given that Juan was moving through the experience in an aimless fashion, racking up debt.

The commonality in these stories is finding a passion – either a reason for being where you are or something that helps you move past where you are.

To paraphrase our friends from IDEO, the famous design and consulting firm that invented the computer mouse, who told us the story about Juan: If you hit a bump, you are more likely to succeed if you know your purpose – why you are there. And that work of understanding who you are is less a finished product at any point in time and more like building a muscle. It requires constant iteration and attention as you evolve. Neglecting it leaves you in a tough place.

Do anything you can to expand your options, see that college is not the only choice at this time, and land in a place that can help you find a passion that drives you into a different Job and whatever it is you do next. Staying put and just going through the motions without actively "shopping" is unlikely to help you turn this stage of your life into one marked by passion, enjoyment, and intrinsic motivation.

WHAT TO DO IF YOU ARE A PARENT OF SOMEONE WITH THIS JOB

- **Do not to be the reason why someone has this Job.**

- **Do not force someone to go to school for its own sake without that excitement, passion, or purpose.** This applies just as much to educators as parents. Parents and elementary, middle, and high schools, for example, should instead intentionally expose students to a variety of career and life pathways and potential mentors to help students build a sense of what they do and don't like, as well as the social capital to help them navigate an increasingly complex world.[4] Cajon Valley Union School District outside San Diego, for example, has its students explore 54 different careers from kindergarten through eighth grade.[5]

- **Instead of forcing your child to go to school when he isn't excited, help your child broaden options.** That might be a gap year, an apprenticeship, a paid job, a coding bootcamp, or even a fifth year of high school. You could also help him find that internal spark that makes the school he does choose make sense.

We know that this is counterintuitive advice. So much of society pushes students to go to college today. But help-ing a student see that there are other acceptable options can be what lifts a cloud from above a student's head and allows her to soar. There is some evidence that students who take a gap year do better when they ultimately enroll in college than those who go straight to college. The excep-tion is if you see that the act of settling will be what spurs your child to finally light the spark that will help her find passion and purpose.

Also, be careful about pushing your child into this Job by forbidding her from applying or going to a place with a high price tag. If your child really wants to go to a certain school, there are ways she can sacrifice to make it work – and there may be unexpected sources of financial aid.

If the student is already in this Job, help her shift into a different Job. Help her shorten her time horizon and find joy in the current school or a place to transfer to. Or you could help her find part-time work while still attending school or grant her permission to drop out and start working. If you do the latter, do not allow her to drop out and do nothing. That is a nonstarter.

She needs to *do* something – get involved in campus life or find work, for example – but that something must be toward building passion or purpose. Helping a student shift into either the Help Me Get into My Best School Job or the Help Me Step It Up Job is probably the ideal next step from where she is now.

WHAT NOT TO DO

WHAT TO DO

Chapter 5

Help Me Get Away

If you're feeling like you need to:

- Get out of a job, role, or habit;
- Get away from your home, town, family, or relationship;
- And/or get a break from the daily grind

So that you can:

- Have the support you need;
- And/or check the box by going to school

Then the Job you may be expecting postsecondary education to fill is what we call the Help Me Get Away Job.

YOUR ESCAPE ROOM

We thought of calling this Job "Help me escape!" But the people we talked to didn't use language that strong.

They said things like, "I gotta get out of here," but not the full-throated cry to escape.

In contrast with the Help Me Do What's Expected of Me Job, people experiencing this Job often struggle to recognize it in themselves.

If at least two of the five bullet points above resonate, and you don't have – or you can't see – any other options beside school, then there's a good chance you're in this Job right now.

Still, saying that you are thinking about going to school to get away may feel uncomfortable. If that's the case, you're not alone. Running from something can be difficult to admit.

The good news is that if you are experiencing this Job and recognize it, then it's easy to be successful. But you have to avoid the trap many people with whom we spoke fell into.

Before we talk about how to be successful in this Job, two stories give a more concrete idea of what being in this Job means.

NAOMI'S STORY

Stepping on the college campus for the first time felt liberating. Naomi soaked in the sights and sounds of the small, picturesque school in the rural Midwest. Three hours away from home and out of range of her stepdad, the possibilities felt endless.

A solid student in high school who did not have to study hard to do well, Naomi only applied to one school. She chose it because a former coworker of hers from Taco Bell was a student there. He told her it had a great atmosphere. As a resident advisor, he knew the administrators well. There were lots of tutoring options, and the advisors were nice, he said.

When she looked it up online, the campus was attractive and the majors interesting. Even though the private college did not have a nursing program – an interest of hers since she had been young – it had biology and health sciences, which felt close enough. The biggest comfort was that she already knew someone on campus, so she wouldn't be alone.

After she got in, Naomi accepted within minutes even though she had never visited. The summer after high school graduation she journeyed to the college for the first time to spend the night.

Naomi's mom did not accompany her on the visit, despite Naomi asking her to. Her mom was busy. She worked as a shift supervisor at the local CVS. She had two other children at home who were 13 and 14 years younger than Naomi. On the days Naomi stayed around the house, she often had to take care of the kids. Naomi's mom had never gone to college, and she did not weigh in on Naomi's college decision. Nor did Naomi's stepdad, with whom Naomi had a bad relationship. Naomi's mom always encouraged her to attend college so that she would have more career options, but at the same time, she hadn't expected Naomi to actually go. Walking around campus without her mom, her mom's two other children, and her stepdad, the sense of freedom was palpable. Naomi felt like she had made the right choice.

KYLE'S STORY

Kyle took a different path.

He had grown up in Alaska, and Kyle had always known that his mom expected that he and his five siblings would go to college. It was understood that you cannot go anywhere without college or trade school or some form of higher education, he said.

But after graduating high school, Kyle did not go to college. He moved into a house in his hometown in Alaska with a bunch of his friends who had also chosen to forgo college. He worked jobs at a big-box retailer and McDonald's.

Because he was in a party phase, Kyle rationalized that college would be a waste of time and money. His mom respected his decision because she understood he did not know what he wanted to do.

On top of that, he and the others in his house were having fun. It did not bother Kyle that he lost contact with his high school friends who attended college. And it did not initially matter to him that the house where he and his friends were living was overcrowded and breaking down.

After a couple years, Kyle's perception changed. He began to notice that his coworkers at McDonald's were younger than he was. Many who had started working after him had moved on to other things. But he was still in the same job. And he and his friends were struggling to make rent. Being near broke – never having money to do anything – had gotten old.

"We were all working retail jobs or fast-food jobs, and, as that went on, I realized that wasn't really working for any of us," he said.

His relationship with his mom was also growing increasingly strained. She wanted him to figure things out and go to college. And Kyle said he was growing sick of living in such a politically conservative state. Then, during a particularly cold winter, the heat in his house did not work. Kyle vowed he was done with Alaska. He needed to get away.

Kyle's grandparents had always joked that if he or his siblings needed a place to crash, they could live with them in their basement in northwest Iowa. Kyle took them up on the offer and moved that summer.

His grandparents took him to the local community college and helped him sign up for his general education classes. The classes were a quarter of the price of Iowa State, Kyle said. They were also smaller, and there was a lot of assistance to help students transfer to a four-year school.

UNDERSTANDING THE HELP ME GET AWAY JOB

If you're at all like Naomi or Kyle, *then circumstances in your life are pushing you to go to college.*

Naomi needed to escape her home life and her stepfather. Kyle needed to get out of Alaska and his dead-end jobs.

Being pushed to do something isn't unusual. All Jobs to Be Done have *pushes* – things that are making us dissatisfied and causing us to look for other options.

In this Job, the pushes are strong.

You likely want to leave a current job, break a current habit, or get away from home and your family, town, or a particular relationship if you are experiencing this Job. You may even be experiencing a mix of these things, as Kyle was.

Or maybe it's less dramatic.

You just want a break from the daily grind. Maybe you want that break just so that you can have some time to think about what's next. That's a normal urge.

Either way, you are trying to get away from something. And like Naomi and Kyle, you probably don't see other options besides school.

The flip side of a push is a *pull*. All Jobs to Be Done have pulls – the allure of something new that causes us to make a change. Without the pull of something new, we stay still. We think we have to do something different, but we don't act.

Understanding both the pushes and pulls of your current struggle is what can help you identify the Job you're experiencing (see Figure 5.1).

In the Help Me Get into My Best School Job, for example, the biggest pulls are having the classic college experience, living in a brick-and-mortar college, belonging to a place with great prestige or reputation, and reinventing yourself with new people. The biggest push is needing to take the next logical step in your life.

In the Help Me Do What's Expected of Me Job, the pulls are weak: using college to check the box and so you can have a safety net. The pushes are stronger: to satisfy or obey people in your life, when you can't see other options, and when you need to take the next logical step in your life.

Figure 5.1 Job: help me get away.

The Top Pushes

- When I need to get out of this job/role/habit
- When I need to get away (from this home/town/family/relationship)
- When I need a break from the daily grind

The Top Pulls

- So I can have the support I need
- So I can check the box

What's notable about the Help Me Get Away Job is that the pulls aren't that strong, either.

You likely want to go to a place where there is a supportive person or two that you know if you are experiencing this Job. Naomi knew a co-worker at the college she attended. Kyle had his grandparents.

And as for why you would attend college, most students with this Job figure they should "check the box" with a degree. Going to college is socially acceptable. You can talk about it with others and feel good about your choice.

Put differently, college – or more school – isn't something that you are striving toward, per se. It just seems like the best way to get away from the pressure of where you are now. It's a good escape valve.

That means that exactly where you go to school is likely an afterthought. How relevant a school's programs are to your passions or likely next step may not matter. A school's reputation or how prestigious it is likely has little to do with the decision you're contemplating.

Most people in this Job are like Naomi and Kyle. Naomi applied to just one school based on the recommendation of her former coworker and a visit to its website. She journeyed to the college only after she got in. Kyle went to the community college near his grandparents because it was affordable and his grandparents helped him register.

You act this way because you're likely not sure about what you want to do after school. Some students in this Job hoped that the experience would help them figure out their passion or purpose. Naomi *said* she was interested in nursing, but the school she attended did not have a nursing program. Being a nurse was not a real priority of hers at this stage in her life.

Acknowledging that you are experiencing this Job before you choose means that you have to be clear in your heart that this decision is really about "getting out" or "taking a break." Deep down, you might not be sure what is next. Your vision of the future is fuzzy. And that's OK.

HOW TO BE SUCCESSFUL WHEN YOU HAVE THIS JOB ARISE IN YOUR LIFE

In fact, it's not just OK. It's normal. Knowing that this is where you are is great.

You need to get away, so do it.

It's not hard to figure out how to make progress in this Job. Get away from what's causing you to be dissatisfied. Take action.

But there are also some risks that in successfully getting away, you might open yourself to some significant downsides. Here's how to avoid that.

Step 1: Know Thyself

Knowing where you are in your life – and where you aren't – is important.

When you're in this Job, **the first step is to be clear about what you are trying to leave, and why.** Be specific. Is it family? A relationship? Home? A job? What it is matters and will impact what is a good choice and what will stop you from making progress.

The second step is to acknowledge that the choice to get away has value – and that you have to work up the courage to get away. You will only make progress once you take that step.

Because let's be honest. Admitting that you have to get away can be hard. And, depending on your circumstance, actually getting away can be even harder.

But acknowledging that this is where you are – because you need a break from the daily grind to give yourself some room to think and figure things out; because you need to get away from home; because you need to get away from work – can unlock tremendous opportunity.

By the same token, acknowledge that you're probably not sure what is next. Be honest that you do not have everything figured out. For example, Naomi realized only after she started attending college that she wasn't ready for the experience. High school had been too easy for her, she said. She had not developed solid study habits and did not know how to work on her own. Kyle's grandparents realized after a semester that Kyle wasn't excited by the community college experience. He enjoyed cutting and dyeing hair instead.

The takeaway? **Not knowing what your strengths or passions are is fine, but given that is where you are,**

before you make a big commitment, use your next step to learn about your strengths and passions, but also your weaknesses and what you dislike.

That means do not overcommit in terms of time and money while you're still figuring it out. Recognize that when you are running away from something but not necessarily toward something, spending a lot of time and money on your next experience is probably a bad idea. Getting away has value, but by getting away, you also open yourself to mistakes that could hurt you. The key is to maximize your exposure to new opportunities that will move you into another phase of your life, but minimize your exposure to downsides and serious risk.

Step 2: Identify Matches

Make sure that all the options you consider actually allow you to get away from whatever you are trying to escape. If you want to get away from home, be like Naomi and Kyle and go to another town. If you want to get away from work, make sure you quit. Of those we talked to who had this Job, 58% of the time they attended school in their town. That means they either chose something that didn't allow them to escape, which isn't ideal, or they were trying to get away from a current job that didn't require leaving town. The main point is be true to yourself. Make sure the options you identify actually allow you to get away from what you need to escape.

Just as important as identifying potential matches in this Job is identifying mismatches. Here are some guidelines.

Don't Bite off More than You Can Chew

Naomi bit off more than she could chew and suffered. She had made the wrong choice in going to college. She was unprepared, didn't have a clear idea of what going to college meant, and yet signed up for an extra heavy course load – 18 credit hours for the first semester instead of the usual 15. On top of that, as many students do, Naomi dove into the party scene. And she paid the price.

When she got her midterm grades back, Naomi knew something was wrong. After first semester, she was placed on academic probation. In her second semester, she declared herself a business major and reduced her course load. Things improved a little. But without a job and with nowhere to live for the summer, the improvement was not enough to justify the money she was spending on tuition, she thought. She still struggled with time management. So with $40 000 in federal and private student loans outstanding, she dropped out, returned home, mended things with her mom, and started to find different jobs to help pay off the debt.

Looking at four-year degree programs may not be a good idea if you are in this Job.

Community college might not be the right fit, either. It wasn't for Kyle. Within a semester, his grandparents suggested he make a change. Given he had little passion for the community college experience but really enjoyed cutting and dyeing his own hair, Kyle's grandparents realized that cosmetology school might be a better fit. Kyle dropped out of the community college and began looking into attending a small, family-run cosmetology school in town.

Over half of the students we interviewed in this Job had left the school they were attending without a degree at the time we talked to them. Fifty-eight percent of people with this Job were dissatisfied with their college experience, and 42% of them went so far as to say that their school had been a waste of time, money, and effort.

Minimize Your Risk until You Are More Certain

Instead of looking to attend school full-time at this stage, as 74% of those who were in this Job did, start by exploring options that allow you to dip your toe in the water with a low-cost, low-risk option that has a short time commitment and allows you to get away. For comparison's sake, because he attended a low-cost community college for just one semester, Kyle didn't incur the extraordinary debt that Naomi did. Still, both could have identified better options that would have lowered their risk profile.

You should not overinvest in yourself when you are not sure what you are trying to do. You do not want to incur lots of debt like Naomi or develop a bad habit without an easy off-ramp.

One of the worst things you can do here, for example, is to attend a state school to get away from mom and dad and then end up just partying. If fun is an important experience at this stage, then you can work a job and have fun. Looking at schools, shopping for classes, and then perhaps skipping them is likely a waste of your valuable time if you are experiencing this Job. There are other instances where it might be OK, but this is not one of them. There is no reason to take out loans and rack up a lot of debt or use up a state's resources at this juncture. It is not worth paying to party in this circumstance; at least earn money while you do it.

Enlisting in the military or joining something like the Peace Corps might not be the right fit, either. Although they will help you get away, those experiences may last too long for where you are. They could put you in a place you do not want to be without an easy off-ramp. And if that happens, you would need to get away yet again, such that you are right back to where you started.

What Are Some Good Options to Consider if You're Trying to Minimize the Downside Risk?

Find short-term or part-time experiences that are affordable – or that pay you. These could include:

- Short-term or part-time educational programs – like bootcamps, a smattering of college courses, adult or continuing education classes, or online courses
- Work experiences – from part-time jobs to paid or unpaid internships and volunteer experiences
- An apprenticeship or career technical program

The idea is to look at options that do not represent major commitments and help you learn what you do and don't like so you can move into one of the other Jobs that might better meet your needs. Shift the emphasis from identifying *schools* to identifying *experiences* that will help you get away and learn more about yourself. That focus on experiences instead of schools is an important step that will broaden your perspective in important ways.

Step 3: Check and Choose

As you get away, learn more about yourself so you have a better sense of what you want to do next – ideally, without spending a lot of time or money.

When we build products and services based on the Jobs we uncover in our research, first we prototype. That means that we build a preliminary model of something so we can develop it further. Then we improve it as we gain information until we arrive at a right answer. In the business world, people often refer to this preliminary model as an MVP – a minimum viable product – that allows you to learn more with the least effort, time, and expense possible. You should adopt the same process here.

This step isn't about figuring out the perfect next step. Instead it's about embarking on a series of quick steps that will help you learn. Build a series of prototypes for your life, as Bill Burnett and Dave Evans recommend in an entire chapter devoted to the topic in their book *Designing Your Life*, to explore questions about what you might want to do by getting some real experience.[1]

Maybe you will learn what you like and start to build some passions, **but even more important is to learn what you do not like.** At the end of whatever you "hire" to do this Job, you want to have a clear articulation of what you do not want to do. And even if you do not know exactly what you like, at minimum, you want to have a sense of what "better" is for you.

Although that means that taking a gap year before going to school might be a good idea, frame it as a series of gap bursts, not one experience stretched over an entire year. A gap burst might last 90, or even 30, days. Having a series of 90-day plans over the course of a year in a variety of experiences would allow you to gain a lot of information about yourself. After each experience, reflect on what you learned in a simple way – "I like more of this, less of that."

Doing a combination of things – taking a variety of educational courses, immersing yourself in different educational experiences, and working a series of jobs that pay and put you in distinct positions – is likely to be informative. And having a job could be a critical way of making money, which would allow you to move away from your current situation and learn about yourself. If you are just sitting around, you are not learning.

Of course, you don't have to follow our advice. Even as the majority of people in this Job didn't enjoy or complete their college experience, many did. That means our advice is not the only way to tackle life when you experience this Job. But if you do follow our advice, it will not hurt you. It will help you establish important guardrails to protect yourself from $40 000 of debt with no degree. It will also help you find a more productive place.

This step is ultimately about transforming a problem – you want to get away but you do not know where you are going – into a learning opportunity. That creates value. The value is getting away plus the set of experiences you gain and what you learn about yourself. Learning how to be alone, paying bills, understanding time management, and developing passions are all critical ways of investing in yourself. They will help you not only complete your Job of getting away, but also help you build a runway toward where you go next.

If you get away and you end up learning five things you do not want to do in your life without spending a lot of time or money, then that is a resounding success.

WHAT TO DO IF YOU ARE A PARENT OF A CHILD WITH THIS JOB

This situation can be tough as a parent, guardian, or close family member or friend of someone who has this Job. As a parent trying to help your child make a decision, you have to recognize that a driving force for your child is that they need to get away from something – and that something may be you. One of us, Bob, is the father of three children who did not complete their college freshman year the year after graduating high school. Recognizing that he had to step back to allow his children to make their own choices was hard – and important. As parents wanting to keep your children safe and help them make good choices, this can be difficult to reconcile. It is critical to acknowledge that a key criterion for success in this Job is that whatever your child does, it cannot happen where she is now.

If you are able to help your child construct an experience that she will hire to fulfill this Job, be clear about what you will support – and make sure that what you support has boundaries. For example, you might help your child move to a different city and then cover all of her living expenses and tuition for educational programs within a specified budget for 12 months. List out some options for what she might do in the city and what you might support – potential bootcamps, jobs, people to whom she could connect to find leads or interview to learn more before committing to something. And create a clear outcome on the back end as a result of your support – some things that she should have learned about herself that she can articulate and parlay into whatever she wants to do next. If college is next, making sure she can pick a curriculum to match her interests might be one way to frame it. The key from a parent's perspective is to help your child gain a lot of experience for not a lot of money while experiencing as much freedom and responsibility as possible.

Structured experiences that give an individual in this Job that freedom and responsibility to learn about themselves over a defined period of time is critical. And if you're the person from whom your child is running, then don't be afraid to confide in one of your friends and have them play a role in helping your child make her decision. Bob calls this the "parent discount," and he uses it with his friend John all the time. The essence of the parent discount is that your children will devalue any advice you offer, but if someone else who is known and trusted offers advice, children often put more stock in it.

Ultimately, for anyone around someone who has this Job, remember the following:

1. Be specific about what's driving someone to get away.

2. Acknowledge that getting away has value.

3. Ensure the individual can act and get away.

4. Help her avoid biting off more than she can chew.

5. Allow her to have experiences in which she can learn more about herself.

WHAT NOT TO DO

WHAT TO DO

Chapter 6

Help Me Step It Up

If you're feeling that:

- What you're doing isn't you, and it's time to get out of your job, role, or habit;

- It's time to step it up because you know you can do better;

- Time is running out to make a change because of some looming milestone in your life, and you're afraid of where things are headed;

- And you know that obtaining some specific, practical skills or certifications can help you take that next step

Then there's a good chance you are looking to go to school to help you step it up.

PICK IT UP

If you are clear about what you want to do next and the steps involved in getting there, then, according to our research, it's also likely that you will be successful. What's important is to make sure you're actually clear about what you want to do. If you aren't, then trouble could arise.

First, to help you understand if this is where you are in your life, we start with Naomi's story from the previous chapter and fast forward five years from after she dropped out of college. We then share two more stories of students who experienced this Job.

NAOMI'S STORY

Five years later, she was back in college.

After Naomi dropped out the first time, she returned home, patched things up with her mom – who was thrilled to have her leave college and come back – and worked a series of jobs to start paying off her $40 000 in student loans.

From Taco Bell, she moved to work at a veterinary clinic, then to a chiropractor clinic as a receptionist, and then started working with doctors and medical assistants in health-care offices before finally working at a hospital. She gradually reduced her outstanding student loan debt to $10 000.

At each turn, Naomi gained more knowledge of health-care practices and the terminology used in health care. She grew closer to her dream of working as a nurse. She began working as a medical assistant and did many of the tasks that nurses would do.

And then she hit a wall. She realized there was no way she could move up at the hospital. Without a bachelor's degree, she could not become a manager or take a more active role in patient care. And she was nearing a salary cap, which was roughly half as much as a nurse would make.

Plus, Naomi's supervisor was an alcoholic. She and her coworkers took the brunt of the supervisor's bad management with no recourse to fix the problem.

Naomi realized it was time for her to step it up. She went back to college at the local university that was a short distance from the hospital where she worked to get a bachelor's degree and fulfill her lifelong dream of becoming a nurse.

NEIL'S STORY

With a decade-long career in information technology (IT), Neil believed he might not need to go back and earn a college degree. There were the tens of thousands of dollars in private student loan debt from his first time in college when he had dropped out that nagged at him every time he had to make his $600 monthly payment. And there was the ever-present voice of his dad, a college dropout as well who also worked in the IT world, who had always struggled with the lack of a college degree. But after feeling insecure for years without a degree, Neil was now feeling established. His hard work was paying off. And he realized if he could get some IT industry certifications, then they could potentially make up for his lack of a degree. He and some coworkers started studying for a certification using some free materials his employer provided.

But then everything changed. He left his job and moved from Chicago to Michigan to be closer to his wife's family. They were thinking of starting a family of their own, so they wanted to be closer to family support. But the move, a house, and a change in jobs were taxing. Neil stopped studying for the IT certification. He said he could not afford it. He also fell behind in his student loan payments.

Neil called the bank where he had consolidated his loans to see what could be done. While on the phone, he learned inadvertently that if he went back to school, he could now defer his loans for up to four years. In Neil's words, this "opened up the field again." He started thinking about what a degree could do for him.

The answer seemed clear. If he was going to have kids, renovate his home, and give his wife some flexibility to pull back from working full-time, he needed to step it up and make more money. Without a bachelor's degree, he had hit a wage ceiling. Although IT certifications could help, having a bachelor's degree would do more. It would allow him to double his salary to $80 000 or even $90 000, he said, by moving out of a user support IT function to working as a network engineer.

Neil applied to a low-cost online program that would do even better – allow him to get a bachelor's degree *and* a host of IT certificates included in the cost. And he could self-pace, so he could move quickly through the program. Within three months, Neil was enrolled in the online university and plowing ahead toward earning a bachelor's degree while continuing to work.

OLIVIA'S STORY

Olivia was feeling stuck. With a master's in education from an elite graduate school of education, she had taught in an elementary school for six years. She loved teaching. But over time, she felt stifled by increasing standardization in her school – mandates around how she should teach a lesson, when she should teach it, and more. It clashed with the educational philosophy that she had learned in school and used in her teaching. By sucking the creativity out of teaching, the administration killed the joy of teaching for her.

After her sixth year, she attempted to switch to become a physical education (PE) teacher. She thought she would have more freedom to practice her teaching craft in the absence of standardized tests. But the school administration stymied her plans. It blocked her move and did not allow her to teach PE.

Shortly after, she suffered an injury playing soccer and had to undergo physical therapy and rehabilitation. The experience was life changing. She wondered if she could practice physical therapy. After talking it over with a friend in the physical therapy field, she quit teaching and started volunteering in a children's clinic and taking prerequisite courses for physical therapy. She applied to the local community college to earn an associate degree as a physical therapy assistant. Once accepted, she enrolled in the fall, one year after leaving the teaching profession for good.

UNDERSTANDING THE HELP ME STEP IT UP JOB

You may be wondering how this Job is different from the Help Me Get Away Job.

If you are in the Help Me Get Away Job, you are focused mostly on escaping your current circumstance. You likely have little sense of what's next. The Help Me Step It Up Job is more balanced between the present and future. It is about moving beyond what you are doing now with a clear focus on what is next.

As opposed to the Help Me Get Away Job where someone is typically trying to get away from a situation or problem, in the Help Me Step It Up Job your focus is on ceasing to *do* something so you can enhance your life. That implies that there are many things about your life you like and want to keep.

Although students in both Jobs said, "I need to leave this job, this role, or this habit," in this Job one of the most common refrains we heard was, "This isn't me. I need to step it up." In other words, I have a problem or challenge, and I am ready to solve it.

That refrain takes on different versions. It could be that you are ready to assume more responsibility, or you decide that what you are doing now is holding you back and you are better than this. Sometimes it is that you are leaving a field entirely – as Olivia did – but often, it is that you are ready to progress within your chosen field, as was the case for Naomi and Neil.

Naomi, Neil, and Olivia all experienced this sense – or need – of having to move on from what they were doing to something better. For Naomi, after having used college as an escape several years earlier, this time she found herself in the position of wanting to progress in her career. Her goal was to become a nurse in order to escape a bad management situation and earn more money. It was time for her to step it up. The outline of Neil's story is virtually identical to Naomi's. He was stuck in his career without a degree and needed to step it up. For Olivia, although the specifics differed – as she already had a bachelor's degree and a master's degree – she found herself in a similar place. She could not be the teacher she wanted to be. In order to progress in her career, she needed to step it up and pursue her next calling. Becoming a physical therapy assistant offered her that opportunity.

The move to action in this Job is generally spurred by some event or shift that makes what you have been doing untenable going forward.

Many of the people we talked to who experienced this Job mentioned that it was "now or never." Time was running out for them to step it up for any number of reasons, from looming milestones like the birth of a child to the loss of financial support or from the threat of being laid off to a sudden struggle of living paycheck to paycheck. Neil, for example, was planning to start a family and renovate his home. Naomi's relationship with her supervisor had reached its breaking point.

If you are experiencing this Job, you likely know what skills or certifications you need to make progress or a fresh start. Naomi knew the precise credentials she needed to become a nurse, how long each would take, and what her career ladder would then be, including when she would need further education. Neil knew he needed a bachelor's degree to double his salary and that he needed the IT credentials to build stability and credibility. Olivia knew she could not become a physical therapy assistant without having an associate degree in the field and passing an examination. She was also clear that she wanted to be a physical therapy assistant, as opposed to a licensed physical therapist, and she understood the tradeoffs in her decision (see Figure 6.1).

The people who experience this Job typically prioritize convenience over the prestige of an institution as they choose their school. Put differently, acquiring the skills

Figure 6.1 Job: help me step it up.

The Top Pushes

- When this isn't me/I need to step it up/I know I can do better

- When I need to get out of this job/role/habit

- When time is running out/it's now or never because …

  ○ I'm facing a looming milestone (e.g., birthday, expecting a child).

  ○ I'm living paycheck to paycheck.

- When I'm afraid of where things are headed (sick of living paycheck to paycheck)

The Top Pulls

- So I can get specific, practical skills/certifications

---

or certifications is more important than where they are earned. This is different from those experiencing the Help Me Get into My Best School Job.

For example, Ken, a student we interviewed, had worked for two years at an advertising technology company. He had been thinking for some time that he might want to attend a coding bootcamp in data science to fill in some gaps in his skillset. After one of his managers took him off an important and interesting project and assigned him to a dead-end position, he realized he had no future at the company. He gave his two weeks' notice and quit – and noticed that a data science course at a coding bootcamp would be starting in just three weeks. Perfect timing. It was not his first-choice of bootcamps, but the convenience – he would not have to wait six weeks to do a three-month program – made it a no-brainer. Ken wanted more experience with advanced statistical analysis, to practice his project-based work, and to leave with a portfolio of code and statistical models to show employers what he could do. He knew the bootcamp he selected would be "good enough" for doing that. Getting quickly back into the workforce with an enhanced skillset was the priority, which is why he did a short, three-month program as opposed to a longer one.

Similarly, although Olivia had earned a master's degree from a prestigious, elite graduate school of education, the local community college that would teach her the skills she needed to pass the physical therapy assistant exam was perfect in this Job. To be sure, she specifically noted that the community college's graduates boasted over a 90% passage rate on the licensure exam. From there, convenience trumped prestige.

More than any other Job in our sample, this one tended to relate to a job – as in, work or career – on both ends. Ninety-two percent of those who experienced this Job had work experience at the time with 28% having an established career. People were often leaving a job and going to school to get another job.

The majority of people looking to hire education to help them step it up were also adults. Fifty-one percent had some college but no degree, and another 36% already had a bachelor's degree.

The Help Me Step It Up Job did not always relate to work, however. And traditional college-age students also experienced it. J. D. Vance, who wrote *Hillbilly Elegy* and was quoted in Chapter 2, had this Job when he graduated high school and decided to forgo college and enlist in the Marines instead. He was not trying to escape home. As he wrote, "I didn't want to leave home. Lindsay [my sister] had just had her second kid, an adorable little girl, and was expecting a third, and my nephew was still a toddler. Lori's [my aunt's] kids were still babies, too. The more I thought about it, the less I wanted to do it."

Instead, he was not the person he wanted to be, and he recognized that college did not make sense. As he wrote, "I wasn't ready. Not all investments are good investments. All of that debt, and for what? To get drunk all the time and earn terrible grades? Doing well in college required grit, and I had far too little of it.... Four years in the Marines, I told myself, would help me become the person I wanted to be."[1] In other words, Vance enlisted to help him step it up.

The Help Me Step It Up Job will also likely occur multiple times in your life. We all struggle through moments in which we need to change something in order to maintain or enhance other parts of our lives that we love. Neil, for example, loved the life he had and wanted to make it even better. But his work and accompanying salary would not allow him to do it. The status quo was not OK.

Importantly, these struggles represent opportunities. *Struggling moments are the seeds of innovation.* More than any other Job we found, the Help Me Step It Up Job is the perfect time to innovate in your life. And we found that the people who experience this Job have significant energy to innovate, as many forces are pushing people to change and pulling them toward a better future.

HOW TO BE SUCCESSFUL WHEN YOU HAVE THIS JOB ARISE IN YOUR LIFE

The odds of successfully completing school are high for those experiencing this Job. But not everyone who hires education to help them step it up completes successfully. According to our research, a significant source of failure occurs when the future is foggy. In other words, if you have not created a clear enough picture of what you want to do next or what is involved in stepping up to accomplish your dream, then it is easy to misstep.

As a result, when you are in this position, it is important to define your picture of the future and then act. Our recommendations help you define what you want to be next as you continue to grow up (and remember, we never finish growing up).[2]

Step 1: Know Thyself

It is hard to know exactly what you want. That is one of the underpinnings of the Jobs to Be Done theory. People often do not know what they want, so we have to look to what people do, not what they say, as well as the energy behind their actions to understand their priorities. Even then, understanding the social and emotional dimensions of the progress you are trying to make can be difficult.

But working to comprehend as much as you can about what progress looks like for you will help you place boundaries on what is good to hire at this stage of your life. To do that, focus on what you like and dislike, your strengths or abilities, and your purpose – collectively known as your abilities and motivation.

Your Likes and Dislikes

Start by taking stock of what you like and do not like in your current or most recent role. You are moving away from something, so what do you want to do more and less of in your next act? Make a list for each. Wanting more money can be part of the equation, but do not just settle for that explanation. Go deeper about all the things you want to change from your current role. Do you want more or less travel? More or less opportunity to manage others? More autonomy or don't care? Part of making more money may also mean doing things you do not want with tradeoffs that are not worth it. Better to know that up-front and take a wider view of what you could do next. Think about what you like in the field you are in and the career you are considering as well. For example, having a physical component to her work became important to Olivia. Working with people to help improve their lives remained a priority.

It is often easier to be clear about what you want to eliminate. That is a great starting point, but do not settle there.[3] Countless techniques exist to help surface what you want more of in your next role and in your life.

Burnett and Evans suggest keeping a "Good Time Journal" in *Designing Your Life* to write down when you feel bored, restless, or unhappy, as well as when you feel excited and focused every day. As you do so, also record what you are doing at those times. You will soon see what engages you, as well as what drains you.[4]

Many recommend the simpler act of journaling. Write for 30 minutes a day, five consecutive days, for example, about anything that comes to mind. More often than not, you will start to write about things that you enjoy and things that you do not enjoy, as well as accomplishments, challenges, and what you have learned along the way. The advantage of a journal is you can admit things in private that you might not want to say aloud.[5]

Working through the *What Color Is Your Parachute* self-inventory is another option, as it takes you through your preferences and priorities in such areas as salary, geographical location, the people with whom you work and interact, the look and feel of where you spend your time, which skills you love, and which fields most interest you.[6]

Your Strengths

Also chronicle your strengths. A lot of our time in schooling and work is focused on our weaknesses. According to Gallup, only one-third of more than 10 million people they surveyed agree strongly with the statement, "At work, I have the opportunity to do what I do best every day." Gallup has found that this has a big cost. A more productive strategy is to focus on people's strengths. According to the book *StrengthsFinders 2.0*, "In a recent poll of more than 1000 people, among those who 'strongly disagreed' or 'disagreed' with the 'what I do best' statement, *not one single person* was emotionally engaged on the job." In contrast, people who get to focus on their strengths at work are "*six times as likely to be engaged in their jobs* and more than *three times as likely to report having an excellent quality of life in general.*"[7]

We both find that taking the StrengthsFinder assessment, which we referred to in Chapter 3 and which you can obtain by buying the StrengthsFinders 2.0 book on Amazon, offers valuable insight into your strengths and can help you focus. There are also emerging software companies that work with employers to help you identify your talents and skills, in addition to your values and interests, in order to help you build your career goals.

Your Purpose

Finally, it is important to think about what your purpose is and why you do what you do so that you can lead your life in concert with that purpose. The notion of purpose can feel like a grand exercise in self-importance and the stuff people talk only about in Ivory Towers, uppity cocktail parties, and professional sports. But it does not have to be abstract, grand, or erudite (yes, we just used that word). The point is to understand what you want to prioritize and make sure you will not live in violation of any deeply held values. This will also help you know what to prioritize when you need to make tradeoffs between the things that you want more of in your life that you identified.

It is true that libraries could be filled with books on the topic of discovering one's purpose. Many of the books have different takes on the question of defining your purpose, so it can feel confusing.

In *The On-Purpose Person*, for example, Kevin W. McCarthy makes the argument that people have one central purpose in their lives. Confusion mounts when people do not have a precise definition for what purpose is relative to vision, mission, and values. "Purpose is being," McCarthy wrote. "It is permanent."[8] The book offers a straightforward and helpful blueprint to discover your purpose. Bob followed the process to learn that he exists to serve by making the abstract concrete. Bob is now able to focus on tasks that help take abstract visions and make them concrete and then leave others to execute from there.

In *Designing Your Life*, Burnett and Evans take a different tact. They see purpose as dynamic. They break down the creation of one's "compass" into two components. First is your view of work – "what it's for and why you do it." We think of this as your goals. Second is your view of life – "your ideas about the world and how it works." We think of this as your view of cause and effect in the world. The magic happens when you combine these to create a coherent vision of what your life should be about right now. In Burnett and Evans's view, purpose will change over time, so you don't have to figure it all out now.[9] Just worry about clarifying your next step. And make sure that as you do so, you understand the social elements of your life – how it connects to others, be that family, friends, your neighborhood, or the world – so you do not neglect that aspect of your life and Job to Be Done. Aaron Hurst, the CEO of Imperative, a career development platform that helps professionals discover, connect, and act on their purpose in their work, has a similar view, as he suggests that purpose "is a journey and not a destination.... To start infusing your work with purpose immediately, take two minutes each day to think of one purpose moment you had that day. If you do this for a month," Hurst said, "you will find that you are doing more things every day that bring you purpose and that you also come to appreciate them more."[10]

In *What Color Is Your Parachute?*, the author Richard N. Bolles suggests thinking about your purpose or mission based on the "spheres" in which you like to be active. The spheres range from those of the senses (having to do with beauty and music) to the body (health, fitness, and care for the weak) and from the spirit (faith) to the mind (truth, knowledge).[11]

Victor Frankl, a neurologist, psychiatrist, Holocaust survivor, and the founder of logotherapy, which is a form of therapy based on the idea that people live in order to find meaning in life, wrote a famous book, *Man's Search for Meaning*, that addresses the topic of one's purpose as well. Frankl suggests that a person's purpose changes over time as a result of one's circumstances, and that we can discover our purpose at a given point in time in three different ways: "(1) by creating a work or doing a deed; (2) by experiencing something or encountering someone; and (3) by the attitude we take toward unavoidable suffering."[12]

For high schools, there is an entire course built around helping students create and clarify their current purpose that IDEO built. Called The Purpose Project (https://thepurposeproject.org), the course helps students clarify their purpose by focusing on a few questions. These questions drive from the earlier exercises we suggest in this section. What are you doing today? What do you like doing? What can you do so that you can get more clarity around what drives you, what you like, and what you don't? Action, in other words, and not talk, clarifies one's purpose. This overlaps with the first way that Frankl says people can discover their purpose.

The ultimate point is to make sure you are true to yourself and not doing something for its mere convenience when deep down inside it violates something central about your identity. It will also help you create priorities and navigate the tradeoffs you have to make between things you like.

Step 2: Identify Matches

After you have gone through the exercises of defining what you want more and less of, your strengths, and your purpose – all of which are connected to each other – the next step is to identify the universe of possibilities for what you could do and then learn about what each would entail. Career coaching can help here, but it is not necessary. The idea is that there are likely multiple things you could do to help you obtain what you want. Expanding your horizons is important because what might seem like a great match on paper might not actually be one when you understand what the path toward reaching it entails or what the daily reality of it is. For example, being a nurse or working in a hospital may sound great, but doing so may require certain changes in your lifestyle outside of work that you are unwilling to make. To expand your options, it is important to brainstorm and generate ideas with a focus on the experiences you need to successfully fulfill your Job to Be Done.

If you feel stuck generating ideas, we recommend the "Mind Mapping" technique outlined in *Designing Your Life* to help. Write down your idea of what you want to do and then, as quick as you can, write down the first five or six related things that come to mind. Then repeat this exercise with each of the five or six ideas you generated. You keep doing this until you have three or four rings of associations, which should greatly expand your horizons of fields or ideas that might be of interest.[13]

We also recommend using your networks of family, friends, and acquaintances, especially those in your outer circles, as another way to generate ideas you might not have considered for what you could do. Reaching out and finding mentors in your community who you do not know well can help. If you have completed the self-inventory Flower Exercise from *What Color Is Your Parachute?*, Bolles recommends showing your friends, family, and colleagues your top three fields of interest and your top five favorite transferable skills to see what jobs those fields and skills bring to mind.[14]

Finally, new apps like Pymetrics (www.pymetrics .com), a career search platform that takes into account an individual's cognitive and personality traits to recommend career paths for job seekers, can also help broaden your horizons.

Step 3: Check and Choose

With the possible matches identified, it is time to understand more deeply what each will entail. That means it is time to prototype.

To learn more about what a new role could look like, you could build a scenario or play out a simulation – even in video games or virtual reality worlds – to learn more. You could try a short internship, use a temp agency to get some experience in what you want to do, volunteer, or sign up for an experience that allows you to immerse yourself in the daily reality of that role. Prototypes should help you learn the path toward each role, as well as the day-to-day experience once you have arrived. What you are looking to understand is, when the high-level appeal of the profession or role is stripped away, are you still excited by the day-to-day?[15] Taking a half step and doing it fully will always be better than taking a full step and doing it only halfway. Do not overcommit before you really know.

For example, say you think you want to sell houses. It is important to understand that to do so, you will have to pass the Real Estate Math Test. Is that a showstopper? In this case, it turns out that there is no penalty for taking the exam multiple times and not passing (outside of the cost). By taking it once without even studying, you can figure out the specific areas you need to work on to pass the exam. That will allow you to optimize your time and figure out if the effort is worth it. You can illuminate the road map. Doing so is important before you enroll in a school without a sense for the subjects you will have to study, tests you will have to take, and time you will have to commit before being able to get the job you think you want.

Similarly, you might be considering a career as a police officer. Sit down and talk to a police officer about the day-to-day routine. You might learn that the daily routine does not appeal to you at all. A next step would be to then go back to Step 2 and say, "What are three things that drew me to thinking that being a police offer would be a good idea?" And then think through what other professions might fulfill those items. Perhaps being a detective or a firefighter would fit the criteria. Doing this exercise before you go to school is important.

Equally valuable is eliminating what you do not want to do. We often saw interviewees in this Job make a mistake here. For example, Mindy, whose story we told in Chapter 2, decided she no longer wanted to work at The Home Depot. Working there no longer represented who she was. She quit and realized within a month that she was ready to step it up and try to prove that she was college material. Prioritizing convenience, she enrolled almost immediately in an online university to become a teacher. Within one month she knew it was not the right fit. She had erred, she said, in thinking she wanted to be a teacher. She wanted to become a midwife. The problem was that the school had no programs with a pathway into midwifery. Going through the three-step process to rule out options, such as teaching in Mindy's case, before enrolling in a school and jumping on the conveyor belt to a particular field is important.

WHAT TO DO IF YOU ARE A PARENT OF A CHILD WITH THIS JOB

Remember, the struggling moment is the seed of innovation. Letting your child – or a friend – struggle can be a great thing because it offers a teachable moment for you as the parent. As the famous book *How to Talk So Kids Will Listen & Listen So Kids Will Talk* says, the way to help children become separate, independent persons is "by allowing them to do things for themselves, by permitting them to wrestle with their own problems, by letting them learn from their own mistakes."[16] A teachable moment can help your child figure out what to do, what tradeoffs she is willing to make, and what to prioritize to set her on a course for life success. The real problem here comes if you help your child or friend avoid the struggle by reducing the friction before she has wrestled with the full dimension of it. Instead, the key is to coach her through it.

As we said, every Job to Be Done has forces that are pushing and pulling people toward making a new choice. Each Job to Be Done also has forces – in the form of anxieties and habits – that are keeping people in the status quo. Using these forces that are acting on your child can help you coach her through her decision.

Start with helping your child home in on what is *pushing* her to change from what she is doing today. You could ask questions like, "Why do you need to switch your paid job? What's wrong with it?" Or you could empathize with her – "I see you feel so frustrated when your supervisor acts like that" – to help her recognize the precise things and moments she does not like.

Then focus on what might be *pulling* her toward something new. "What could possibly be better than what you do now? Why is that good?" Or "You seem happy when you get to work with the children in the hospital."

Next focus on what is holding her back. Start with what is *creating anxiety*. "What are you worried about?" If your child says something like, "Well, I don't know if I can do the work if I get in," you can dig into that further. Maybe your child is right – but maybe not. For each answer, do not be afraid to ask "Why is that?" five times to help her understand her underlying anxieties.

Finally, dig in to why your child might be *reticent to leave what she is currently doing*. Ask questions like "What do you have to give up to make this progress? Why is that important?" Empathize with comments like, "I can see that you really like how well you know your colleagues in your current job."

The idea is to support your child or friend as she moves through the three-step process outlined above without forcing her there by helping her understand how to make progress. What's critical is to help make the tradeoffs in your child's decision explicit. Whereas the Help Me Get Away Job has few tradeoffs to be made, this Job has a lot of tradeoffs because no move to help someone step it up is going to be perfect. People will have to prioritize based on life circumstances and what they are trying to preserve. Surfacing those tradeoffs is critical so your child can make a wise decision, given her present circumstances and likely future. That means helping her understand clearly what she is going away from and what she is moving to.

WHAT NOT TO DO

WHAT TO DO

Chapter 7

Help Me Extend Myself

If you are looking to:

- Learn more and challenge yourself;
- Pursue a clear vision for yourself;
- Earn specific, practical skills or certifications;
- And at last you are ready – with the time and money to get more education

Then you are likely looking for school to help you extend yourself.

LEARNING FOR LEARNING'S SAKE

Of the five Jobs we discovered, this one is perhaps the most about learning for learning's sake. It's the ultimate Job in lifelong learning. If you're experiencing it, you're likely excited to enrich yourself with knowledge and skills.

But it's not just about enriching yourself. Those who experience the Help Me Extend Myself Job are longing to accomplish something that is meaningful to them. In contrast to the Help Me Step It Up Job, they aren't running from something. Things in their life are good, and they now have the time to tackle a vision they are driven to pursue.

Given the intrinsic motivation embedded in this Job, it's unsurprising that the vast majority who experience it express satisfaction at the end. Our advice is designed to help you avoid the twin risks of overcommitting and paralysis – and to make sure you maximize the opportunity in front of you.

We start with three stories that exemplify this Job, so you can recognize it in yourself.

NAVEENA'S STORY

With a master's degree in communication management in hand, Naveena was enjoying her first year as an account manager at a company in Silicon Valley. Still, she had a habit of checking LinkedIn for interesting job postings during her down time, and she occasionally applied for positions.

As she surfed LinkedIn for postings, she was drawn to one opportunity in particular. It had data analytics at its core. Even though she had no background in data analytics, Naveena had grown excited about the field after working with a data analytics client. With an affinity for numbers, she regretted that she had not studied a more quantitative field in college or graduate school. She wished someone had talked to her about how important her major would be to her future opportunities and what her day-to-day work would look like. The notion of working with numbers and problems that would be more "black and white" appealed to her.

She applied for the position. To her surprise, things moved quickly. The company brought her in for a couple of interviews. Soon she received a job offer. It contained a substantial pay increase and the opportunity to do more data-oriented work. The company also trained all its employees in-house, so Naveena would be able to start building her data analytics skills. She was thrilled.

After thinking about it for a week, Naveena went back to her current company and told them about the offer she had received. To her surprise, her company counteroffered. Even though it did very little with data at the time, the company expressed excitement about building a data capability in-house because "everyone was working with data these days," Naveena said. Her company offered Naveena a pay increase, the opportunity to transition over the next six months and start the company's data analytics department, and – the gravy on top – the opportunity to attend a training program to build her skills. The company would cover 100% of the tuition, so long as she made a commitment to stay for at least two years.

Within a week, Naveena had made her decision. She would stay at her current company. The next step was to find a suitable training program. She did a little research before choosing a coding bootcamp that she had heard a lot about in the past. It seemed to have instructors who were professionals active in the data analytics field. She cleared things with her company over the next month and then jumped into a "quick and easy" three-week enrollment process before starting a week later in a part-time program.

TRISHA'S STORY

We met Trisha in Chapter 4. Experiencing the Help Me Do What's Expected of Me Job, she had attended a Christian college in Tennessee and ultimately dropped out. After that experience, she tried college a few more times, but never graduated. Several years later, she finally felt ready to tackle college. This time would be different, she thought.

She did not need to go per se. She had been living with her boyfriend for a few years now. He had a stable job as a firefighter. They did not need the income. And with a two-year-old at home plus four other children from other marriages, continuing to stay at home and run a household would not be a bad thing, she reasoned.

But she also wanted an occasional break from the kids. And more importantly, she wanted her children to see that once you start something, you finish it. "I wanted to have that personal achievement," she said. "I wanted to be able to say, 'I started, and it took me forever to achieve my goal, but I finished.'"

After an adulthood of instability, some extra security would not be a bad thing. She signed up for online courses at the local community college so that she could take and pass the math courses required to gain admission to an occupational therapy assistant (OTA) degree program.

Because of her own health issues – she had significant back problems lingering from her pregnancy – she had no idea if she would end up working as an OTA. But she knew that to have a chance, she needed to pass the online courses. And if she and her children could see that she was making a difference – "not just for [her family], but for other people who have needs" – it would all be worth it, she said.

KAREN'S STORY

With most of her peers in nursing starting to retire, Karen realized that she, too, could retire at any time. But she wasn't ready. Her work was not done.

A leader in her field for three decades, Karen had founded a post-partum/lactation outpatient clinic at her hospital that was the first in the country to receive a special UNICEF and World Health Organization certification. As age 60 neared, Karen knew that if she retired, she was secure financially. But she wanted to make sure that the clinic she had started and still ran would not fade away. So she committed to staying for another decade to create a training program for up-and-coming nurses so that the clinic would run smoothly after her retirement. She wanted to provide those nurses with the same type of mentorship she had received early in her career.

On top of the need to leave a legacy, she felt determined to get a master's degree in nursing. After earning her Bachelor of Science degree in nursing in the 1970s, she had learned she was pregnant. She pulled out of a master of science in nursing degree program to focus on family. As her career progressed, her husband discouraged her from ever enrolling because it did not seem worth the money.

But after divorcing her husband of 40 years and with her children out of the house, she said she now had the time to chase that degree. And earning an RN-MSN in Nursing Leadership would help her to leave the lasting legacy she desired by helping her put the right processes in place in her hospital. Yes, she was nervous – she had been out of an academic setting for so long – but she was ready for the personal challenge. Everything was lining up for her to get that master's at last.

UNDERSTANDING THE HELP ME EXTEND MYSELF JOB

We originally thought about calling the Help Me Extend Myself Job "Help me enrich myself." Those who experience this Job, however, have a yearning to accomplish something that is meaningful to them that the word enrichment doesn't capture. They are not meandering.

- **If you are experiencing this Job, you likely want to learn more and challenge yourself.** There are different flavors of this. Naveena longed to enter the data analytics field and make numbers a daily part of her job. Trisha sought to prove to herself that she could finish what she started years before and be a role model for her children. And Karen wanted to complete a master's degree she thought she should have always had and use the knowledge to benefit the program she created at her hospital.

- **If you are experiencing this Job, you probably know what skills and certifications you need to make progress as you pursue a clear, concrete vision.** You are seeking to learn something and become something more. Naveena knew what the bootcamp program would teach her and open up for her career-wise. Trisha knew she needed to pass the online math courses to get into the local community college's OTA program. And Karen had a clear sense of her future at this juncture in her career. She was not ready to retire, and she knew that she could use the projects she would complete in the master's degree program to help her create a lasting legacy at her hospital. Almost everything she would learn would have relevance. More than a certificate or degree, people with this Job want the knowledge, the challenge, or the doors that a badge recognizing their accomplishment may open. It is all about improving you.

What differentiates this Job from the Help Me Step It Up Job is that the status quo is OK. People with this Job are not saying, "This isn't me," or, "Get me out of this role." Naveena is enjoying her current role. Trisha is in a stable place where she does not need to go back to work at that time. And Karen could retire but she wants to keep going and preserve her legacy.

As a result, the decision to enroll in an educational program is relatively low risk. If you experience this Job, enroll in a program and do not complete, and then you go back to where you were, there is little downside. Little risk means different things in different circumstances, of course.

A friend of ours who had been the CEO of a large, publicly traded company experienced this Job and attended divinity school at a major university to fulfill something he had always wanted. Although for some that would be a big risk because of the commitment in time and money, after having been a CEO, the risk was low for him.

Bob experienced this Job when he attended Stanford's design school (known as the Stanford d.school) to learn more about design thinking and connect it to the Jobs to Be Done theory. It was a full-time program where you were supposed to live on-campus. Bob told Stanford he could not move to Palo Alto from Detroit to attend full-time. Given he did not need the degree – he just wanted the learning – he asked what other options were available. If Stanford had said there were no other options, there would have been little downside to his career. (Bob's negotiation worked, as Stanford ultimately said he could enroll part-time through its executive education program.)

When unearthing this Job, Michael wondered if he had ever experienced it. He ultimately realized that every time he reads a book to learn more about education or cognitive science, he is experiencing this Job. His current living situation with two young daughters and a mortgage to pay have dictated what he must hire: books and podcasts that have a short time horizon and are low cost rather than a full-fledged degree program. The following observations are consistent with this experience:

- **A line we often heard from people in this Job was what Karen said: Now I have the time to do this.** This was true for virtually everyone in this Job. People were emotionally ready to achieve their goals – many of them lifelong ones.

- **They now had the time, money, and freedom to do so.** Naveena's company paid for her to extend herself and created time – and a transition period – for her to do the bootcamp program. Trisha was in a stable place where she finally had the time. Our friend who had left his CEO post had the time to pursue his passion. And when Michael dives into a book, he has the time and budget for that learning experience.

The elements pushing you in this Job are fairly passive: you now have the relative time and money to pursue more education. This Job is instead almost all about the pull of the new – the allure. It's about what the learning will get you or the learning itself. If you're experiencing this Job, you're intrinsically motivated (Figure 7.1).

This Job often occurs when life is under control and things have slowed down. People often use online courses or, when they are on a shorter time horizon, books or podcasts to fulfill this Job. Even a vacation or a conference can be something someone hires to do this Job. As opposed to the Help Me Get Away Job that likely occurs only a couple times in your life, this Job occurs a fair amount, especially

Figure 7.1 Job: help me extend myself.

Top pulls

- So I can learn more/challenge myself
- So I can pursue a clear, concrete vision
- So I can get specific, practical skills/certifications

Top pushes

- When I am ready now/at last
- When I have the time and can fit it into my life/schedule/budget

---

if you hit a certain point in your life and you have more time to invest in yourself.

The majority of people who experienced this Job had work experience – 79% – and 46% had an established career. The majority also paid out of pocket for the education that they chose – meaning they didn't rely on loans, an employer, or anyone else to finance their education.

One distinct persona also emerged from our research: moms in their 40s, 50s, and 60s. Like Trisha and Karen, they had often skipped or dropped out of an education program earlier in their lives, the memory of which stayed with, and even haunted, them. Because life got in the way – kids, paying bills, work – they had been unable to enroll. These moms had unfinished business. When they at last had the time – as Trisha and Karen had – they seized it and enrolled. They did so to prove to themselves they could successfully complete more education, and sometimes, like Trisha, they did it to be a role model for their children.

HOW TO BE SUCCESSFUL WHEN YOU HAVE THIS JOB ARISE IN YOUR LIFE

Perhaps because it was low risk and they now had the time, a whopping 87% were satisfied with the experience they chose.

If you try a new experience and do not love it, it's no big deal in this Job because you can go back to what you were doing before – and you can still be satisfied with having invested in yourself.

If you complete whatever educational experience you choose, the upside is supreme satisfaction. This Job is ultimately more emotional than social. You are doing this for you. The work you do will build your confidence as you progress through a set of learning experiences.

As a result, the key in this Job is to focus on maximizing your success and the opportunity in front of you – and making sure you don't overcommit or fail to commit at all.

Step 1: Know Thyself

Realize where you are. You now have the time and money to pursue an educational opportunity that you want. Be honest about what that means for you. Exactly what time are you willing to commit to this? What tradeoffs are you willing to make? How much money can you responsibly commit to paying for this experience?

What you want to do in this step is clarify your boundaries so that you can both maximize this opportunity by committing fully, but also not turn it from a low-risk opportunity into a high-risk one by burning bridges, spending too much, or making unacceptable tradeoffs for your current life. Remember – you're OK with what you have right now. Don't lose sight of that.

Step 2: Identify Matches

First, given that there is little push in this Job and it is almost all about the pull of what you could learn or be, broaden your set of what you could hire. Make sure you shop and find the right fit. Be creative. This is all about bettering yourself – whether that is seeking enrichment for your life, in parenting, or in the job market. If you think an online program is the right fit, think about other possibilities and substitutes as well. Consider your full range of options within your risk profile.

Second, as you shop, do not turn this from a low-risk point in your life to a high-risk one. Do not consider options that would cause you to overcommit and put yourself in a high-stakes place – say, taking on $75 000 in debt up-front in a situation where that is an inordinate amount of money for you. Look to take lots of sips, no big gulps.

Step 3: Check and Choose

The biggest advice in this step is to make sure you choose something. There is a real risk of paralysis in this Job – that you stay with what you are doing currently and choose to do nothing new because life is good. You owe it to yourself to overcome that.

Do not let the habit of the present hold you back before you have hired something. Reduce your anxiety around trying something new by reminding yourself that you can always go back to what you were doing if what you hire to extend yourself does not pan out.

Then grant yourself permission to try something. The most likely risk when you have this Job is that you opt for the status quo and hire nothing. You do not need something new, but it is a great way to round yourself out and shoot for something you have always wanted or about which you have become curious. With your basic needs taken care of, you've earned the right to learn more and explore your potential.

As you choose, be willing to negotiate with the educational programs you are considering. If you are experiencing this Job, then life is OK. Do not get pushed into doing something that is not appealing. You do not *need* to do anything; you *want* to do something. Remember, if Bob was able to negotiate with Stanford, you can negotiate, too. Make sure what you choose here is as appealing as it can be. There's no reason to settle.

Finally, do not burn bridges with what you were doing. After all, you may go back to your former habits if the new is not as appealing as you had thought it might be.

WHAT TO DO IF YOU ARE A PARENT OF SOMEONE WITH THIS JOB

Given that the real risk for people in this Job is that they do nothing, if you are a parent, friend, or colleague of someone who has this Job, tell that person to go for it.

Help her see that she has little to lose so she should push past her current habits. Help her see that she can be picky and that she can negotiate.

Negotiating can be hard. Having someone behind you is tremendously helpful. And give permission. Say, "You can do this." Encourage her to be a lifelong learner and explore.

One student, Sybil, had never completed her high school degree. She was employed, had two children, and, after some rocky years, settled in a comfortable place in her life. She also saw many of her colleagues from work attending the local community college, which she drove by wistfully every day to work.

One day she was telling a colleague about how she had been a good student and had a thirst to learn more. Her colleague encouraged her to enroll by saying, "Now I think you could do it. It's never too late." Then she told Sybil about how when she had gone to college, there had been a woman enrolled in her 70s who had put her children and grandchildren through college and now it was her turn. Sybil realized, "You know what? There is nothing holding me back right now." She enrolled a short time later.

This was not uncommon. In our interviews, people often told us that someone had given them permission to move beyond what they were doing currently. Having someone help reduce their anxiety around doing something new was critical for helping them realize that they could dive in, get more education now, and extend themselves.

Do not minimize your role. Give people in your life with this Job permission to reach higher and extend themselves within their means.

WHAT NOT TO DO

WHAT TO DO

Chapter 8

Living Life Through the Jobs

Naomi and Trisha's stories show that not only is it possible to experience more than one of these Jobs in your life, but it is also almost a certainty.

The students we talked to who attended more than one postsecondary program experienced many of these Jobs – and they often circled back to Jobs they had already experienced multiple times. As you've read, maybe you've noticed that you have experienced many of these Jobs as well. Bob has.

BOB'S STORY

As we shared in Chapter 4, Bob did not get into his dream school when he was a senior in high school. He fell into the

Help Me Do What's Expected of Me Job and attended the local regional university where he was accepted. He was not pleased about it. He was aimless and unsure why he was there. He felt like he did not fit in.

Almost immediately upon enrolling, Bob moved into the Help Me Step It Up Job. Living life in a listless and aimless state wasn't him. He was determined to do something about it. He did not hire a school, however, to help him make progress. Instead, he found a part-time job at the Ford Motor Company as an assistant engineer. He loved it.

He wanted to drop out of school and work full time, but his boss told him that Ford would not hire him full time without a degree. With a clear motivation and understanding of what he needed, Bob was – within a matter of a few months – in the Help Me Step It Up Job for a second time. He committed fully to the college, graduated, and started working full time as an engineer.

While stationed in Germany with the Ford Motor Company several years later, Bob found himself in the Help Me Extend Myself Job. There was nothing wrong in Bob's life, but he wanted to deepen his knowledge of the business side of Ford's operations so that he could design better products. That meant starting to understand strategy, marketing, and sales. He enrolled in Boston University at Brussels, as did his wife, and the two of them commuted for a year to Brussels on the weekend. Bob took business classes to extend himself. Taking the classes wasn't going to result in more money. He was not worried about getting good grades or how he performed on the assignments. He just needed to understand the concepts being taught and be able to use them. Bob never completed the program, but he enjoyed the experience.

After returning from Germany, Bob moved into a new role as a vice president at American Supplier Institute, where he worked on improving the speed and success of developing new products. The new role required that Bob move from tactics to strategy, which required him to step it up. He needed to prove himself. He enrolled at the Massachusetts Institute of Technology and studied under Dr. Don Clausing, the former head of innovation at Xerox, so that he could make the grade.

After a little over four years at American Supplier Institute, Bob founded a new consulting firm to help companies with their product development, sales, and marketing in the food and beverage industry. Two years later, with better ability to control his time, he again experienced the Help Me Extend Myself Job. He recognized that his clients had bigger problems that he wanted to help them tackle. He enrolled in an executive education MBA program at the Harvard Business School so that he could gain knowledge to extend himself and help his clients. While at Harvard, Bob worked with Professor Clayton Christensen on developing the Jobs to Be Done theory and began helping more companies develop products and services that would satisfy customers when they were struggling and didn't have a solution.

Bob's career progressed from here. And then in 2012, 15 years after leaving the Harvard Business School, he found himself back in the Help Me Extend Myself Job. With the growing popularity of the Jobs to Be Done theory, alongside the growing popularity of design thinking, a problem was emerging. Although people constantly connected the ideas, they typically misapplied one or the other when doing so and therefore lost out on the insight. It was clear to Bob that the concepts should be linked to each other – and that he could take the principles of design thinking to extend the utility of the work he did with Jobs to Be Done. But he did not know enough about design thinking to understand how. So with a problem in mind, he applied to the Stanford d.school for a Master of Science in Industrial and Product Design.

As we recounted in Chapter 7, Stanford accepted him into the two-year program and said he would have to move to Palo Alto, California, to enroll. But Bob could not just pick up and uproot his family members from their location outside Detroit. Because he was in the Help Me Extend Myself Job, not the Help Me Step It Up Job, Bob realized the degree was not a necessity. His life would be OK if he did not enroll. So he started negotiating with Stanford. He asked to do the degree part-time – meaning it would take four years, not two – and that he wanted to do it from a distance where he just flew in to work on the projects. Stanford said that he could not do that through its traditional program, but he could do it through its executive education program.

FIVE PRINCIPLES FOR YOUR LEARNING JOURNEY

Bob's life story helps us see five general principles about the journey you will take through these different Jobs.

1. You Will Experience These Jobs Multiple Times

You will experience these Jobs many times in your life. In just this short detailing of Bob's career and education, Bob experienced the Help Me Step It Up Job and the Help Me Extend Myself Job three times each.

He has almost certainly experienced both many more times. For example, Bob has the Help Me Extend Myself Job several times a year. Sometimes he hires a conversation with Clayton Christensen to make progress. Other times he might enroll in a free online math class from MIT to help him extend and improve the math used in his Jobs to Be Done work. Similarly, many people may experience the Help Me Step It Up Job when it is time for them to move on from their current employment, but they do not necessarily need more education to help them make progress. If they leverage their expertise and network, they can simply switch employers or jobs. Bob actually hired part-time work – a position at Ford – to help him make progress the first time he experienced the Help Me Step It Up Job.

2. Your Options Are Broader than School

A key takeaway is that school, or even an informal education program, is not always the answer to the progress you are seeking when you have one of these Jobs. Understanding the Job you have changes your possibilities.

In the Help Me Get Away Job, for example, getting away is critical, but entering full-time school probably doesn't make sense. Likewise, when Bob revisited his decision to attend Boston University at Brussels, he realized that if he were in that circumstance today there would be many more affordable and convenient services available – from online videos to personal tutors – to hire instead of a university.

Critical to achieving your personal success is correctly identifying which Job you are in and then deciding accordingly. It would have been easy for Bob to think that once Stanford admitted him to a master's program, his only option was to go along with how the program operated. It was *Stanford*, after all. Implicitly understanding that he was in the Help Me Extend Myself Job, however, allowed him to see that missing out on the educational experience was preferable to moving to Palo Alto full time and hurting his family life. Given that the brand and the degree were not what he was after – he wanted the knowledge, and it was not mission critical – he was in a position to negotiate and find a viable option.

3. Each Job Operates under a Different Time Horizon

One trick for recognizing which Job you are experiencing is to understand the time horizon under which you are operating as you make your decision.

- **In the Help Me Get into My Best School Job, your time horizon is getting into school. That is it.** It is about winning the "game" of school and gaining acceptance, less about what you will do once there. This Job is often punctuated with the phrase, "I can't wait to get to school," with students viewing that once they are in, they will be set. Once there, many will of course ask, "What now?"

- **In the Help Me Do What's Expected of Me Job, the time horizon can feel undefined.** If you are feeling listless about attending school, however, and think you have been pushed to attend, then shorten the time horizon and think in terms of months, not years.

- **In the Help Me Get Away Job, your time horizon is very short.** You are seeking to get away. Once you have accomplished that, you will have made the progress you need to. Remember, in both this Job and the Help Me Do What's Expected of Me Job, you are being pushed to attend. In the Help Me Get Away Job, that push is internal, whereas in the Help Me Do What's Expected of Me Job, it is an external, social push.

- **In the Help Me Step It Up Job, two things govern your time horizon.** First, because of some event, you feel that you have to act now or never. And second, your time horizon is measured by what you are seeking to step up to. For example, if it will take two years of education to earn a credential and get the new position at work you desire, that is your time horizon.

- **The time horizon in the Help Me Extend Myself Job is defined by your risk tolerance.** It could be anything from a matter of days – if you only have time to read a how-to book, for example – or years, if, like Bob, you can enroll in a four-year, part-time program. You also have made this Job a priority in your life such that now you have the time to tackle it and can fit it into your life and schedule.

4. Once You Choose, Your Job Shifts, Too

Bob's story shows that the moment people make a decision about what education to consume, their circumstances can change. They might have a very different Job to do that is now bounded or informed by the educational service they just hired. Once Bob made the decision to attend his local regional university, for instance, he shifted from Help Me Do What's Expected of Me to Help Me Step It Up while he remained enrolled.

We call this phenomenon the "Big Hire–Little Hire." The "Big Hire" is the moment you buy a service – in this case, when Bob enrolled. But there is an equally important moment: when you actually consume it. The moment a consumer has made a purchase, oftentimes that service then sits waiting to be hired over and over again – what we call the "Little Hire." For example, when you buy a shirt, what is now important is whether you decide to wear it and why. Or when you buy a phone, which apps do you buy and download? And how often do you use them?

Once enrolled in an educational institution, the classes you choose (and which ones you actually attend), the work you do, the clubs you join, and the college services you use are similar. This book does not focus on that aspect of the educational experience after your initial choice, but it is clear that understanding those Little Hires – the subsequent Jobs to Be Done – is what helps you unlock the value in your experience. Bob's ability to take the requisite courses at his local regional university so he could graduate to step it up and get a full-time job that excited him were vital.

As you understand what an educational experience actually offers once you have enrolled, your Job will shift. And the Jobs you experience will likely go far beyond the five we've explored in this book that occur when people are making the decision whether to enroll.

5. Your Learning Journey Will Last a Lifetime

Finally, learning is a lifelong endeavor. That has always been true, but it is an economic necessity today. As the shelf life of skills shrinks and the durability of degrees declines in the face of rapid discoveries, technological advancements (such as automation, artificial intelligence, and machine learning), and job changes that remake our economy, individuals are under increasing pressure to move beyond a one-and-done approach to learning. The dean of Harvard's Extension School, Hunt Lambert, argues that we are increasingly embarking on a personalized "60-year curriculum" with multiple pathways throughout. Adults will have to reskill far more frequently.

That means we will constantly consume education – formal and informal – in our lives in unexpected ways and in unexpected circumstances. Being clear about those circumstances and the outcome we are trying to accomplish is critical to making smarter decisions to get the right value from the experience.

Part

Helping Educators Design Better Choices

Chapter 9

Why Understanding the Job Changes What You Offer

We've concluded the section of the book dedicated to helping potential students make better education choices. What follows in the next two chapters is written for the people who offer education programs to help them design better offerings that are more attuned to the reasons that students are attending. If you are a student or parent, you can stop reading now and skip to the conclusion for a few parting thoughts that bring our advice to you and our advice to education providers together.

Of course, reading the next two chapters won't hurt you – and they can help. They can help you know what to look for to see if schools are acting with your Job to Be Done in mind. But it's not required reading to get value from this book.

APPLYING THE JOBS TO YOUR JOB

In this chapter, we dive deeper into the logic behind the Jobs to Be Done theory to help education providers think differently about how they structure their offerings, as well as the design of their organization. In Chapter 10, we offer specific pieces of advice for providers.

If you work at a college or university, lead another type of education program, or plan on starting one, at this point you're likely wondering: I see how understanding the Job you're experiencing can help a prospective student, but how can understanding these different Jobs help an institution or an entrepreneur?

The short answer is that if you understand the *causal* reason why people are doing something, it's easier to create a solution that helps them make progress. As you design, build, and deliver, you can take into account people's circumstances, harness their motivations, and help them achieve what they are chasing.

In this chapter, we use some language and examples from the business world to illustrate four classic traps that people fall into when they design a service, as well as how the Jobs to Be Done theory helps avoid these traps by focusing on causation, not correlation. We then show how understanding people's Job to Be Done can help you change what you offer and the structure of your organization so that you consistently prioritize the progress people are trying to make in their lives. Although the business world is very different from education, by offering examples with some distance from the world of education, we hope that it will enable you to distill some of the central insights from the theory. In this and the chapter that follows, we also offer many examples from higher education so that you can see how the ideas apply.

WHY NEEDS, DEMOGRAPHICS, CATEGORIES, AND LISTENING TO USERS MISLEADS

In every sector, more than 75% of all new products and services fail. In your own life, you have probably experienced frustration as companies take an established and beloved product or service and add features that are, at best, irrelevant to you or, at worst, make the service more complicated to use and more expensive. From your perch at an education organization, you have likely been frustrated as prospective, current, and past students gave you feedback that did not seem to improve your program's outcomes.

The reason for these struggles is not because organizations have forgotten to collect enough data or listened hard enough to their customers. We have more "big data" than ever before and yet the professionals designing products and services miss just as often. Organizations similarly spend more hours and dollars on focus groups and innovative ways to listen to their users and customers in an effort to improve what they offer. They load up on features, luxuries, discounts, and glitzy marketing messages. Yet the swings and misses keep on coming.

Organizations miss because the common techniques for creating something new fail to capture the *root causes for why* users consume and the actual context in which they do so that forces people to make tradeoffs.

As individuals, we typically just find ourselves having to get things done. We all have *jobs to be done* in our lives – *the progress that we are trying to make in a particular circumstance*. The choice of the word "progress" is intentional. It represents movement, or a process, toward a goal or aspiration. A Job is rarely a discrete event. It is also not necessarily just a "problem" that arises, although it can be. As the stories of students deciding to go to college show us, sometimes people hire college to solve a problem they are facing and make progress in their lives, and other times they are just hiring it to make progress with no pressing problem in sight. Either way, as we've seen, the decision is a process.[1]

There are at least four classic mistakes that organizations make that contribute to the swings and misses:

1. **They believe that just because people "should" do something because of a "need" in their life, they will.** Organizations often fall into the trap of thinking that just because a service appears beneficial to a customer, the customer will embrace it. In particular, organizations with a social mission, such as those with an education, wellness, or environmental-protection objective, often launch services that don't take off even though their solution is irrefutably worthwhile and addresses a "need." For example, after the US Department of Agriculture updated its school lunch guidelines, cafeterias across the country replaced pizza with fresh vegetables. But as lunch trays got healthier, the number of students purchasing school lunches took a nosedive.[2] Nutritious eating is not a goal most children have, even if they "should" do it to be healthy.

   Importantly, a Job to Be Done is different from the traditional design thinking or marketing concept of "needs." Needs always exist in someone's life, but they fail to capture what someone is prioritizing in a particular circumstance. They therefore miss what will motivate people to take action and what tradeoffs they are willing to make.

Just as many people deprioritize maintaining their physical health even though it is something they need to do and should pay attention to, many students languish in school, do not enroll, or do not come to class at all because education itself is not a Job that they are trying to do. As we've seen, education is something they can choose to hire to do their Job – but it often is not the Job itself. What that means is that teachers can work extraordinarily hard to improve the features of a class in the hope that more engaging lessons, media, and student-response clickers will improve student motivation. But their efforts are in vain if they are aimed at providing an even better way for students to do something that they were never trying to do in the first place.

The graveyard of failed services is filled with things that people should have wanted – if only they could have been convinced those things were good for them.

2. **They group people by demographics.** Organizations often group people by demographic categories, such as "millennials," "stay-at-home moms," or "iGen students." The problem is that from an individual's perspective, the world isn't structured by customer category. Lumping people together by surface-level characteristics that correlate only loosely with the different circumstances and challenges individuals face leads organizations to build one-size-fits-all offerings that serve few well.

The segment between the ages of 18–34 is often used in consumer marketing, for example. But it lasts 17 years – during which time attitudes, behaviors, circumstances, and priorities change dramatically. Demographic data cannot explain why someone takes a date to a movie on one night but orders in pizza to watch a movie from Netflix the next. Which is better? It depends on the circumstance.

Most colleges and universities behave as though the world is structured by customer category. Each college knows the exact demographics of its student population – age, gender, race, marital status, first-generation college, income level, and more – and often accordingly tailors its offerings.

3. **They design initiatives to fit a category rather than to address people's circumstances.** Once they frame something as part of a category of similar services, organizations then tend to load up on all the "right" or "best" features of that category without addressing the actual circumstances people are struggling to improve. Many colleges and universities behave this way. They compare themselves to peer institutions in a particular category, such as research universities, state and regional colleges, community colleges, and more. They then copy many of the features from their peer institutions.

The problem is that from an individual's perspective, the world isn't structured by product category. People are typically looking for something to help them make progress in a particular circumstance. We often mistake products and services for the result that someone is actually seeking. In the case of those who have the Help Me Get into My Best School Job, this is ironically in many ways true, but it's the exception, not the rule. As the famous marketing professor at Harvard Business School, Theodore Levitt, once said, "People don't want quarter-inch drills.... They want to buy a quarter-inch hole!"

But even that is incomplete. Why do they want the quarter-inch hole? Do they want to hang a picture to impress their friends? Or change some wiring in their house? The *circumstance* someone is in defines what success is and the tradeoffs that person is willing to make. Quality is not absolute, in other words. If we are trying to court a high-net-worth potential donor, treating her to a meal at a high-end steakhouse might be ideal. But if we are hosting a second-grade team's end-of-year soccer party, it would be a disaster. A pizza joint would be a much better bet.

4. **They listen to what people say rather than watching what they do.** Countless experts and books suggest we should listen to what people say and build accordingly. The counterintuitive reality is that, without meaning to, people frequently misrepresent what they want. It's not that customers lie intentionally. The problem is that they don't actually know what they want.

Consider innovations in the textbook industry. During market research interviews, students and their teachers expressed enthusiasm for books that included links to websites where they could learn more about topics covered at only a cursory level in the books. In response, textbook companies spent millions of dollars creating websites where students could explore topics more deeply. As it turns out, however, very few students ever click on those links. What most students really are trying to get done in their lives – as evidenced by what they do, rather than what they say – is simply to pass the course without having to read the textbook at all.[3]

It is ultimately not a customer's job to innovate. That is an organization's job. And as an organization, it is more important to watch what customers do, not what they say.

MOVING FROM CORRELATION TO CAUSATION: WHAT JOB DOES A MILKSHAKE DO?

If these four common techniques cause organizations to misstep as they design, build, and deliver a service, how does the Jobs to Be Done theory avoid these traps?

A story helps illustrate.

In the mid-1990s, a fast-food restaurant chain was trying to improve the sales of its milkshakes. Its marketers first defined the market segment by *product category* – milkshakes – and then identified the *customer demographic* – working-age adults – who historically bought the most milkshakes. Next, the marketers *invited people who fit this profile to focus groups to collect feedback* on what sorts of changes would improve the shakes. Should they be thicker, cheaper, or chunkier, for example? The panelists gave clear answers, but the consequent improvements to the product had no impact on sales.

The restaurant then turned to Bob Moesta for help. He took a different approach. *Rather than ask customers how to improve the milkshake, he spent several days in one of the restaurants for 18 hours at a time to observe what*

was taking place anytime a customer bought a milkshake.
He took copious notes. What time of day was it when
people bought a milkshake? What were they wearing?
Were they with anyone else when they bought it? Did they
buy anything else? Did they drink the milkshake inside of
the restaurant or go off to their cars and slurp it down as
they drove off?

Bob was surprised to find that nearly half of all milkshakes were purchased during the early morning rush-
hour commute. These customers were almost always
alone, they did not buy anything else, and they went
promptly into their cars and drove off with their
milkshakes.

After analyzing the results, Bob returned and essentially confronted the customers as they left the restaurant,
milkshake in hand, and asked (in language that they
would understand), "Excuse me, but could you please tell
me what Job you were trying to do when you came here
to hire that milkshake?"

As they struggled to answer, he helped them by asking,
"Think about a recent time when you were in the same
situation, needing to get the same Job done, but you
didn't come here to hire a milkshake. What did you hire?"
Most of them, it turned out, bought their milkshakes to
do essentially the same Job: they faced a long, boring
commute and needed something to make the commute
more interesting. They weren't yet hungry, but knew that
they'd be hungry by 10 a.m.; they wanted to consume
something now that would stave off hunger until noon.
And they faced constraints: they were in a hurry, they
were wearing work clothes, and they had (at most) one
free hand.

In response to Bob's question about what other products they hired to do this Job, the customers realized that sometimes they bought bagels to do the Job. But bagels were dry and tasteless. Spreading cream cheese on the bagels while driving caused serious problems. Sometimes these commuters bought a banana. But bananas didn't last long enough to solve the boring-commute problem, and the commuters were starving by 10 a.m. Doughnuts were too sticky and made the steering wheel gooey. The milkshake, it turned out, did the Job better than any of these competitors. It took people at least 20 minutes to suck the thick milkshake through the thin straw, which gave them something to do with that free hand while they drove. They had no idea what the milkshake's ingredients were, but that did not matter to them because *becoming healthy was not the Job they were hiring the milkshake to do*. All they knew was that at 10 a.m. on days when they had hired a milkshake, they did not feel hungry – and the shake fit cleanly in their cup holder.

Bob observed that at other times of the day, parents often bought milkshakes, in addition to a complete meal, for their children. What Job were the parents trying to do? They were exhausted from repeatedly having to say no to their kids. They hired milkshakes as an innocuous way to placate their children and help them feel like loving parents. But Bob saw that the milkshakes did not do this Job well. He saw parents waiting impatiently after they had finished their own meal while their children struggled to suck the thick milkshake up through the thin straw followed by inevitable temper tantrums as parents threw out half-consumed milkshakes and dragged their screaming kids back to the car.

Customers in the same demographic were hiring milk-shakes for two very different Jobs. But when marketers had asked a busy father who needs a time-consuming milkshake in the morning – and something very different later in the day – what attributes of the milkshake they should improve on, and when his response was averaged with those of others in the same demographic segment, this had led to a one-size-fits-none product that did not do either of the Jobs it was being hired to do.

HOW UNDERSTANDING THE JOB CHANGES WHAT YOU OFFER

Understanding this dynamic, how would we improve the milkshake to help an individual accomplish the morning rush-hour commute Job or feel like a loving parent? Figure 9.1 shows the three levels in the architecture of a Job we'd need to consider. Getting each of these levels right can help you build an offering that nails the Job to Be Done. Not coincidentally, it also follows the scaffolding from the earlier chapters of how we structured our advice to students to help them be successful, as we took them through a three-step process of knowing

Figure 9.1 Architecture to successfully design for a job to be done.

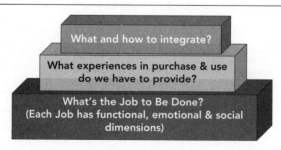

What and how to integrate?

What experiences in purchase & use do we have to provide?

What's the Job to Be Done?
(Each Job has functional, emotional & social dimensions)

themselves, identifying matches based on the experiences they wanted, and checking and choosing to make sure what they chose actually delivered on those desired experiences.

At the foundational level is the Job itself – the fundamental progress the customer is trying to make in a particular circumstance and the result that the customer must achieve. For many morning commuters who hire milkshakes, the Job is to mitigate the boredom of the long drive and stave off morning hunger. As we've observed throughout the book, Jobs are not just about making progress along functional dimensions, like staving off hunger. Jobs also have social and emotional dimensions, which are often more important than the functional ones. In a confounding way, they are also harder for customers to articulate. For the afternoon Job where customers hire the milkshakes with their kids, the social and emotional dimensions of the Job are significantly more important than the functional considerations, for example. And in the case of going to college, the social and emotional reasons behind someone's decision often weigh far more heavily than any functional considerations.

The second level in the architecture is composed of all the experiences in purchasing and using the product or service that its vendor must provide, so that they add up to getting the Job done perfectly. For the morning rush-hour commute Job, that would mean understanding what customers with this Job must experience as they learn about this milkshake brand for the first time. What about when they are making the purchase each day? And then when they get in their cars to consume it, what should that experience be like? Should the milkshake be more viscous or more fluid? Healthy, unhealthy, or doesn't matter? In a paper or plastic cup?

The final level in the architecture of a Job stems from an understanding of what experiences a service must provide to deliver on the Job. This allows you to integrate properly by knitting together all the right assets – human resources, technologies, ergonomic features, packaging, training, support and service capabilities, distribution and retail systems, and branding and advertising strategies – that are required to provide each of the experiences necessary to do the Job perfectly. For the morning rush-hour commute Job, that would mean making the shake even thicker so that it would last longer. Swirl in tiny chunks of fruit so that the drivers would occasionally suck a chunk into their mouth, which would add a dimension of unpredictability and anticipation to their monotonous morning routine. Just as important, they could move the dispensing machine in front of the counter and sell customers a prepaid swipe card so that they could dash in, gas up, and go.

If the chain wanted to improve milkshake sales for the Job of helping me feel like a loving parent, then it would have to repeat the same three-step analysis and design a very different offering. A one-size-fits-all solution will not work. Ultimately, and perhaps counterintuitively, **understanding the Job – more than understanding the customer – is what matters.**

ORGANIZING AROUND A JOB

Understanding the Job to Be Done helps organizations design better services for specific circumstances. Organizations in industries notorious for high prices and poor customer service are almost always integrated incorrectly to help customers get a specific Job done. We suspect that the managers of those organizations think that they are integrated properly, in that each element that is required for customers to buy and use their product or service exists. But the elements are not knit correctly together to do the Job.

Colleges and universities provide a perfect example. They are typically organized by academic field: departments of mathematics, physics, French, economics, classics, and so on. The reason for structuring universities in academic departments is to facilitate the faculty's ability to interact with others who share common interests and expertise and to help them publish in specialized academic journals so that they can earn tenure. As a result of these structures, college education for many students entails repeated bouncing back and forth in a cumbersome way between departments and administration to get their education. And colleges incur extraordinary overhead expenses – what are called administrative costs – to deal with the fact that few of them are organized in ways to optimize the flow of students through the requisite experiences. It is no coincidence that colleges and universities are caught in a world where they are slammed increasingly for providing an overpriced service that does not give students what they really want – and yet leaders at those same college campuses bemoan how society misses all the value they provide.

IKEA

Contrast that example with the retail giant IKEA. The company presents a case study in understanding the Job and organizing successfully to deliver a solution for that Job.

The Job that IKEA has focused on is to help people furnish their apartments *today*. Many of us may remember having that Job when we landed in a new city after college, for example.

Understanding this Job, IKEA engages its own designers to create furniture kits that customers can retrieve from the warehouse, take home, and assemble themselves, without having to wait for delivery. IKEA designs furniture that is explicitly meant to be temporary, not to become heirlooms. IKEA offers childcare because unfettered concentration on furniture purchases is an important experience, and it stations an affordable cafeteria in the store so customers can refuel.

What is so interesting is that by understanding the Job it does so well, IKEA has remained impervious to competition. Anyone can walk through its stores and examine how IKEA works its profitable magic. Yet no one has copied it. Instead, most retailers organize their businesses around a customer segment – wealthy individuals, for example. Or they organize around a type of product – say, modern furniture for those living in cities.

IKEA does not do any of that. And because it is focused on nailing a specific Job to Be Done, IKEA understands what improvements will help it do the Job better and what will prove to be distractions.

As a result, IKEA still sells low-cost furniture today, a half century after its founding. It has not gone "upmarket," as most businesses and colleges seeking to be "better" do naturally. Nor has someone come underneath IKEA to push it upmarket, despite all the disruptive innovations (meaning innovations that transform a market by offering something simpler, more convenient, and more affordable than what previously existed) in retail, from discount to online to low-cost providers in China – where, incidentally, understanding customers' particular circumstance has led IKEA to integrate forward to help deliver and assemble the furniture as well.

Southern New Hampshire University

This playbook hasn't just been used in the corporate world. In higher education, Southern New Hampshire University (SNHU) adopted the Jobs to Be Done thinking to redesign its school.

Several years back, SNHU's President, Paul LeBlanc, realized that the university was in essence serving students with at least two different Jobs to Be Done. Using the language of our research, one was the student who was hiring college to Help Me Get into My Best School. Students here were focused on things like sports teams, climbing walls, and interaction with faculty around the meaning of life. The second Job LeBlanc noticed was that many adult students SNHU served were in the Help Me Step It Up Job. Students in this Job cared about things like convenience, customer service, speedy completion times, and credentials. They were hiring SNHU's online program, which the university had historically treated as a side project.

As LeBlanc's team dug into the Jobs to Be Done theory, it realized that it was treating these students with very different Jobs the same. For example, SNHU began talking to traditional high school students about basic financial aid information their junior year. Not having specifics for at least a year worked fine for both the student and the university. Any student inquiry would take weeks to resolve because there was no urgency on either side. But for students in the Help Me Step It Up Job, they needed answers on financial aid right away. Their time to act was now or never. Waiting hours, let alone weeks, to respond was too late. What had to change at SNHU? "Pretty much everything," LeBlanc told the authors of the book *Competing Against Luck*. Students in the Help Me Step It Up Job needed quick responses to inquiries about financial aid. They also needed to know whether previous college courses would count as credit toward an SNHU degree within days. SNHU redid its advertisements for its online programs to focus on the training students needed to advance in their career, but also the emotional and social dimensions around the pride one feels in realizing a goal. When asked in an advertisement why they earned their degree from SNHU Online, one father said, "I did it for you, bud," and held back tears as his young son said, "Congratulations, Daddy!" SNHU realized that it was not enough just to enroll students, but it had to support them to and through graduation. SNHU Online assigns students a personal adviser, for example, who stays in constant contact with students and picks up on red flags even before students do in many cases.

This undertaking also changed how SNHU measured success. For example, SNHU would have formerly measured how it responded to student inquiries in terms of how many packages were mailed out. It would then wait for the interested students to call. But now SNHU Online measures response time in minutes. The goal is to call back in under 10 minutes.[4]

Getting the Organizational Structure Right

Colleges, universities, postsecondary education programs, and entrepreneurs starting up programs must address what the different Jobs to Be Done mean from a design perspective and adjust their operations accordingly.

To deliver successfully on a particular Job to Be Done, an existing institution may have to rethink everything – much as SNHU did. That can be challenging. SNHU, for example, had to move its online program to a separate unit outside of the governance of its core campus program so that it would have the autonomy to rethink the processes it used to serve students and the division's priorities. For some colleges, it may mean less drastic changes. And for those starting brand-new programs, they have a blank slate to get it right.

Either way, institutions must rethink not just the service they provide but also their fundamental organizational structure. That means tearing up the notions of who reports to whom and focusing instead on how different parts of the organization interact so that they can deliver on the Job to Be Done for which they are being hired. Building predictable, repeatable processes so that an organization can integrate properly around a student's Job and then engraining those processes in the structure of the institution is imperative.[5]

Of course, this assumes that you know *what* to do to serve people in each of the Jobs to Be Done we identified. Helping you know what you should offer to better serve students in the Jobs we identified is the topic of the next chapter.

Chapter 10

How Institutions and Entrepreneurs Can Design Better Experiences

WAYFINDING ACADEMY'S STORY

A new school in Portland, Oregon, is flipping the college script. Rather than focus on majors and degrees, Wayfinding Academy, a two-year school, spends time on self-discovery – who you are now and where you go from here.[1]

Most of its students already tried college and found it did not work for them. The required classes did not make sense to them, and they were not sure why they enrolled.

According to Wayfinding Academy's founder, Michelle Jones, a former professor at Concordia University, that is not unusual. "Our culture of higher education is backwards. We first ask young people to first pick a four-year university to attend, and then to choose a major from some list, and then to figure out what they want to do, and then to go try it. And I feel like we need to flip this frontwards."

At Wayfinding Academy, although students take academic classes, they also meet at least twice a week with a "Guide," a college official who blends the roles of career counselor, life coach, and academic advisor. One of the meetings is one-on-one, and the other is with all of the Guide's advisees.[2] Students spend a significant amount of time outside of the school as well in internships, trips overseas, and with mentors. Everything is designed to make sure students leave with a purpose by helping them get out into the world before they find their place in it. Even the academic classes are engineered to help students figure out who they are, as every student takes nine required classes in social change, leadership, team-work, and communication. Students ultimately graduate with an associate degree in "Self and Society,"[3] but more to the point, the Wayfinding team hopes, a sense of what they want to do next. To that end, students graduate with a digital portfolio of 8 to 10 items that reflect who they are and what they can do. At a price of $10 500 per year, Wayfinding Academy says it does not measure success in degrees or debt.

Whether Wayfinding Academy will succeed is uncertain. The school breaks the traditional higher education mold in several ways. Although the school is not accredited yet, Oregon's Higher Education Coordinating Commission has approved it to offer its associate degree. No one yet knows if Wayfinding Academy's program of self-discovery will work, and whether the school can create a sustainable business model while paying all its employees the same, relatively low salary. There is also a real question of whether enough students and families will trust it to enroll for two years. True, its program appears designed to help students answer questions that emerged in our research as critical ones. For students looking to hire a school to help them step it up because what they are doing now is not them, Wayfinding Academy could be the perfect path for clarifying what they want to do next. But given the urgency for people with this Job to step it up, will Wayfinding Academy produce the outcome they need at the end of the program? The questions Wayfinding Academy seeks to help students answer also seem perfect for students in the Help Me Get Away and Help Me Do What's Expected of Me Jobs. But will a two-year program that costs $21 000 still be too long and cost too much for someone who is hiring school to help them get away? Will someone who is just looking to do what is expected of them go to a school that does not fit society's or most parents' expectations?

We will learn the answers to these questions in the years ahead. But what Wayfinding Academy is doing is fundamentally rethinking the higher education experience. Based on our insights around why students hire college, it is a useful experiment given that most colleges and universities were not built around students' Jobs to Be Done. As we wrote in the previous chapter, delivering successfully on a Job to Be Done is what causes customers with that Job to be satisfied and willing to pay premium prices. It also allows organizations to streamline what they offer and be more efficient by reducing administrative overhead costs. This matters because administrative costs at colleges and universities have risen significantly over the last few decades and outpaced the growth in students and faculty by significant margins.[4]

What follows are some insights into how postsecondary education programs should optimize for each of the different Jobs. We do not have all the answers. We invite campus leaders, entrepreneurs, designers, and researchers to help us understand what postsecondary institutions should do so that we, along with others, can publish more insights. What institutions and startups can do today, however, is take the insights from this book as a foundation and enter into a design process to create prototypes and other experiments that test assumptions to see what does and does not work in reality and in their context, learn the right lessons, and then adjust and iterate accordingly. Finding a safe place to undertake this design process that does not interfere with a program's core operations and the students it serves today is wise.

COMPARING THE FIVE JOBS

What emerges from the Southern New Hampshire University (SNHU) example in Chapter 9 is that students in these different Jobs often need fundamentally different experiences to be successful and satisfied. Colleges that offer only one service are unlikely to be able to serve students in all the Jobs well. Standardization – the notion that colleges should look alike and adopt similar processes – will only create one-size-fits-none offerings. Focusing on each Job and creating the right opportunity will be important to be successful in the long run.

That means that many colleges will need to make hard choices. They will need to identify which Job they should be serving. That choice will, in turn, dictate what they must be good at doing – and, by definition, what they should be intentionally bad at doing.

To illustrate the point, what is noteworthy is that students in the Help Me Step It Up Job and Help Me Extend Myself Job have a reasonably clear notion of what they want out of their educational experience. They are focused on an outcome. For students experiencing the Help Me Get into My Best School, Help Me Do What's Expected of Me, and Help Me Get Away Jobs, they are trying to figure it out. They are focused on the act of getting to an educational experience. They will then take life from there. Even the students who know what they want to be – say, a doctor or a lawyer – and want to get into their "best" school to pursue that vision are still focused at this stage on getting into the school. Once in, they will focus accordingly on the pre-med set of courses, for example, to position themselves for medical school. Understanding these simple differences has profound implications for how one should serve these Jobs.

Another way of seeing some of the differences in the Jobs is to imagine a math major that has each Job:

- A student in the Help Me Get into My Best School Job may just be saying, "Help me get my math degree from Yale."

- A student in the Help Me Do What's Expected of Me Job is saying something like, "My mom said I was good at math, so I am taking it."

- A student with the Help Me Get Away Job majoring in math says, "I'm good enough at math. I'll major in it to get me out of where I am today."

- A student with the Help Me Step It Up Job may want to be a data analyst because it pays well, and she sees that majoring in math will be a ticket to that role.

- And a student in the Help Me Extend Myself Job has an interest in math because it will help her better serve her existing clients or because of a deeper curiosity in mathematics. The student is intrinsically interested in the subject itself.

Just because all these students said they will major in math does not mean all colleges should be accepting them all as math majors.

GO BEYOND THE AVERAGES AND SURVEYS

Jobs-based thinking also allows us to start going beyond averages to understand why certain interventions, programs, or features may help *some* students be successful but *not* help – and maybe even hurt – others. In one recent report on online learning, for example, 57% of respondents said interacting with their peers and faculty is important to them. What should a university do with this information? Although a little over half said interaction was important, a sizable 43% said it was less so. Understanding what Job the students have when they hired the educational institution – along with information about students' prior knowledge in the subject matter, for example – would help tease apart the different results.[5] For students in the Help Me Extend Myself Job, for example, where the reason for learning is personal, interaction may be less important than for those experiencing other Jobs.

In other research we did, a regional public research university was trying to figure out its competitive edge over the nearby flagship university in its state. One thing it discovered was that many students who chose it over the flagship did so because they valued the regional university's "community" feel as opposed to the "active campus life" at the flagship university. The leaders puzzled over what this meant. As we unpacked it with them, we saw that many of the students attending the regional public research university had the Help Me Step It Up Job. The school's reputation for providing a supportive *community* and helping make sure that people got where they wanted to go regardless of their background were assets in that journey. The active campus life of the flagship university – top-ranked sports teams, a thriving college town, and an active Greek life – were far less interesting to students in the Help Me Step It Up Job. But for those with the Help Me Get into My Best School Job, those assets were a significant advantage.

With that as backdrop, here are some thoughts on serving students with each of the different Jobs.

HELP ME GET INTO MY BEST SCHOOL

Many colleges will argue that they have a significant leg up when it comes to this Job because what a lot of students are buying is the classic college experience that they have been led to expect. In many cases, those colleges are right.

Despite survey data that suggests exorbitant expenditures on climbing walls, dining halls, and the like are not what students want, our research suggests that for many students in this Job, this may very well be exactly what they want – so long as it meets what is best for them.

The existence of this Job suggests that despite its rapid growth, online learning will not replace the brick-and-mortar, residential college experience anytime soon, if at all.

And in the debate about having *fixed course sequences* versus the "beauty" of allowing students *to explore from a wide variety of courses and stretch intellectually through the liberal arts*, choice, breadth, and depth will likely continue to win out for many students with this Job.

There are a few cautions and pieces of advice, however.

This Job has several segments lurking within it that vary by persona. Students who know they want to go to medical school or law school, for example, may have a very different flavor of this Job from those who want to go to school to party. Institutions should dig deeper to understand exactly what is pulling students to them so that they can optimize accordingly. If you delve into a robust Jobs discovery process, you are likely to discover nuances that will cause you to structure your institution in different ways and invest in different areas. This would also help schools focus and differentiate themselves.

To that end, many colleges are becoming more expensive yet undifferentiated and unfocused. In a world of unlimited resources, many students and their families might continue to opt for these programs. But most students and families do not live in such a world. With limited resources and questions around the future of work, they may voice skepticism about the value of these expensive, undifferentiated institutions and look elsewhere. Demand for traditional college experiences is unlikely to be infinitely inelastic. Indeed, many small, rural liberal arts colleges are already on the precipice of closing, as their business model is fundamentally unsustainable.[6]

Following from that, **there is likely a limit to the number of colleges that can win at this Job.** Already today only a minority of college students lives on campus and is enrolled full time. That number will likely shrink in the years ahead given changing demographics that will result in far fewer traditional college-aged students.[7] Many colleges probably think they are serving students in this Job, but are in fact being hired to Help Me Do What's Expected of Me or Help Me Get Away. It is important to be realistic about the circumstances in which your students actually are, not where you wish they were.

Finally, **entrepreneurs may struggle to serve students with this Job** because, by definition, students are seeking the best school for them. The outcome is, to a certain degree, defined by the solution. But opportunities still exist.

Entrepreneurs could create new programs that make the college experience far more affordable, focused, and robust – like what the Minerva Project, the first elite liberal arts college to launch in over a century in the United States, is doing.

One can also imagine entrepreneurs creating programs that unbundle the elements of a prestigious college experience. Students could have opportunities to reinvent themselves and meet new people as they travel abroad, live in communities with their peers, and work on Habitat for Humanity or company projects. They could learn academics online and on-demand or in blended-learning bootcamp-type settings. And they could gain access to prestigious networks of people in a range of professions desirable to them through membership in various societies and clubs.

Although this may sound far-fetched, given that access to baseline knowledge and experts is becoming increasingly affordable and accessible paired with the rapid increase in the fundamental cost of college and the number of employers beginning to say that they will not require a degree for certain positions, this may be more possible in the years ahead for many students. Sure, the most elite institutions will likely be fine, but the question is, how many institutions are in that elite category with the resources to allow any student, regardless of their financial means, to be able to pay for an increasingly expensive experience?

HELP ME DO WHAT'S EXPECTED OF ME

Accepting students who are in the Help Me Do What's Expected of Me Job places an institution in a tough position. In many cases, students here have fallen from the Help Me Get into My Best School Job to this one, or they are adrift and just following external pressure to enroll in a school. They often, but not always, lack a purpose. Our advice for institutions centers on helping students compress their timeline and move into a new Job.

An institution could help prospective students see when its educational experience is not a good fit for the progress the students are trying to achieve and the circumstances in which they find themselves. Counseling students into a gap year could make sense, for example. If they do this, however, schools should only counsel students into gap year programs where the travel a student does or set of experiences the student has are focused on *doing* something, not just passively absorbing an experience or having fun for its own sake. The idea is to help students grow up by flipping them from trying to do what others expect them to do to what they expect themselves to do. The question is: what experiences do students need to help them move to and through that flip?

Helping students go through those experiences in an expedited manner that does not waste their resources is the right thing to do, but is not always in the narrow economic interests of the school that may benefit from having students attend and pay tuition for longer periods of time. Schools should overcome that short-term economic temptation. It is not in the long-term interests of anyone. Instead, the purpose of a gap year for students in this Job is so that they can build passion and purpose, and the school can showcase its relevance to what students learn they want to do. After a year, the students would ideally come back to the school fired up and ready to embrace the experience.

There are other options. **Institutions could embrace who they are serving and lower the expectations around the experience. For example, institutions could market themselves as "The Transfer College," a stopping ground on the way to a student's "best" school.** Some students, like Maddy who we met in Chapter 4 and attended a nearby school from which she could always transfer after her first-choice school deferred her, might discover that they do not want to transfer. Their best school is right where they are. Other students might embrace the support that an institution provides to help them find the right match, along with the support in preparing them to be admitted and succeed at that "right school."

Alternatively, institutions could help students shorten their time frame for making a decision about what to do next after enrolling by creating a program in the first semester that helps students build a purpose – and then helps students decide whether to stay enrolled, get a job, do a gap year, or transfer to fulfill that purpose. The program could focus on helping students understand their abilities, where they desire to make an impact, and their passions by helping students catalog what they already do and what they want to explore – as well as how that all fits with potential life pathways and in-demand opportunities.[8] From there, students could create project plans, execute those plans, reflect on the experiences, and discover patterns – and then repeat the process. Over time, this intentional experimentation will help students build a purpose. As the IDEO Purpose Project high school course on the topic states, "The more you do, the more you discover what you like and what you don't like . . . . so there's less noise and more you."[9]

Entrepreneurial educators have lots of opportunities here that others likely do not. The challenge will be to help students – and their families or support networks – widen their view beyond college of what they could do next and then enroll them in programs that help them build passion and purpose or consciously move them into a new Job.

HELP ME GET AWAY

If you are at a multiyear institution and accept students with this Job, our first piece of advice is to **revamp your general education or first-year program.** Students with this Job often do not know what they want. They are running away from something. **Helping them build passions, but also figure out what they do not want, is what is important.**

Wayfinding Academy appears to be building for this Job. The same is true for the many community colleges that have created "guided pathway" programs. Guided pathway programs attempt to redesign the entire school experience starting with helping students identify their career goals in the beginning of the program. They then offer clear maps that guide students through their course of study so students do not, for example, take courses that don't count toward their degree. This last part is important because racking up a lot of debt when students are unsure of what they want to do can be reckless and wasteful if it unintentionally prolongs their college experience. Although it may bring in revenue for the institution because students stay longer, it does so in a perverse way. And it creates an opportunity for new organizations to emerge that offer more successful programs for students with this Job.

The question is whether this kind of thinking is enough. Many of the institutions offering guided pathway programs still accept students into a specific "meta major" and then help them figure out which program within a cluster of options will be best. Students with this Job may not be prepared to even make that decision.

Furthermore, many of these community colleges still require that students take traditional general education requirements that have arisen out of the academy, like English and math. There is a question of whom this is benefiting. Will students need the first-year mathematics? Without students knowing what they want to do, institutions can't know, either. **Colleges should work with their** faculty, accreditors, and state authorizing associations to rethink the general education course sequence to match the experiences students in this Job need to be successful.

But thinking in terms of courses – as opposed to offering experiences like short immersive sprints through different fields – may *still* fall short. Courses plus presentations by professors and companies that help students learn about different fields – as happens in many guided pathway programs – may suffer from a Goldilocks problem in helping students gain a true picture of whether a pathway is right for them. They either will not be enough for a student to figure it out or may be overkill. For example, although some community colleges wisely use a course to help students who think they might want to be a phlebotomist – people trained to draw blood from a patient – learn whether they even like touching people before venturing down the full path of required courses, does a student really need a whole course to figure that out? There are surely more efficient ways to chunk the experiences involved in being a phlebotomist to help students decide quickly if it is right for them.

In other cases, offering immersive experiences or bootcamps in different fields may be far more effective at helping a student understand what a career path will really be like than a simple course and a presentation or two from someone in the field. Duke University, for example, has begun creating mini-bootcamps to make sure students have the same basic skillset before a course begins.[10] Duke has been successful in bolstering students' knowledge before they jump into a course. But these mini-bootcamp experiences also have the advantage of making sure students know what a course of study will really be like and whether they are attracted to the subject before they take a whole course in it – let alone commit to a major with a set sequence of courses, as in guided pathway programs. **Students with this Job ultimately may need a series of directed short explorations of different fields, not a fixed sequence of learning within one field.**

If institutions choose to serve students in this Job, then they should also make sure that students have one strong preexisting relationship to support them on campus. Although students were running away from something when they enrolled in this Job, most said that they went somewhere where they knew they would have a familiar face and someone to support them.

More to the point, traditional schools should consider whether they are best fit to serve students in this Job. Perhaps they should instead, as in the Help Me Do What's Expected of Me Job, **encourage students to enroll in gap-year experiences that allow them to benefit from a series of short experiences that immerse themselves in a variety of fields and help students move to another Job.** This is less and less unusual today. Schools as highly ranked as Princeton and Tufts offer formal bridge-year programs for students before they enroll.[11]

Colleges shouldn't stop there. They should consider partnering with some of the programs, like Global Citizen Year or Winterline, that offer structured gap years to offer financial aid as well as credit for the experiences and demonstrated learning that students accumulate.[12] For low-income students in this and the Help Me Do What's Expected of Me Job, this could be the difference between a gap year stretching into years of struggling through low-wage jobs just to pay the bills and an on-ramp into a productive life pathway.

Alternatively, **entrepreneurs and schools could create their own short-term, gap year, or bootcamp-type programs that allow students to prototype a variety of career and life pathways to figure out what they do and do not like.** Students could earn a certificate or other credit at the end of the program. But more important is that the programs offer students a chance to get away and learn about themselves without requiring that the students overinvest in themselves at this stage, given their uncertainty.

HELP ME STEP IT UP

Students in the Help Me Step It Up Job typically come to college motivated and ready to move forward in their lives. This is a powerful place for institutions to serve students.

Guided pathways or other programs in which students move through a clear, fixed set of learning experiences that result in their desired outcome – a better job, for example – are ideal. The choice students require is which program to attend, not which individual courses they should take once they are enrolled. Traditional colleges have historically offered students lots of course choices. A broad range of choices, distributional requirements in a range of disciplines, and standard general education requirements will generally be a poor fit for students with this Job. They will often be unnecessary, and they could also be harmful, as they could cause students to have challenges getting into the courses they need for their major, take courses they do not need, and therefore graduate late with additional debt. Once students in the Help Me Step It Up Job are enrolled, they want the most direct path to getting the learning and credentials they need to move up in their lives. Any clutter will annoy and hamper the students.

Creating programs that are convenient, accessible, and "good enough" to step it up are what matter. Prestige and high-end brands for their own sake do not matter in this Job. **Having multiple start dates might be critical, for example, so that a program is more accessible given that students in this Job want to start as soon as they are ready.** If stepping up in a given field means that someone needs a credential, then students are looking for that. If they just need the learning, then that is what they are chasing. Understanding different students' pathways to step it up outside of schools – what do employers require, for example – will allow a program to focus on the specific experiences that students in this Job need.

The two dangers lurking for serving students with the Help Me Step It Up Job are if students have not crystallized their vision or they have an inflated sense of their abilities relative to the specific field of study. As a result, schools serving students in this Job should consider making the three-step process we suggested students do in Chapter 5 part of their application process to ensure that students applying truly know who they are and what they are trying to accomplish given their current circumstance. That means asking students to define who they are – what do they like and dislike, what are their strengths, and what is their purpose; articulate which life options match their profile; and paint a clear picture of what they want to do next. If students pass convincingly – they show that they really know who they are, what they want to do next, and have a clear vision of what it will entail – then lay out for the students what they will have to do to step it up. Make all the requirements and work in the program explicit. If students are ready, then they can enroll and jump on a defined pathway. Although this type of application may sound difficult, making an application "harder" can actually build energy so that the students enrolling are fired up coming into the experience. We often use energy in designing things to build this pent-up momentum for a service.

If students do not pass the application, then they need to go through some type of process similar to what we discussed in the Help Me Get Away Job where they work through a series of short experiences that immerse themselves in different fields along with a set of exercises around their strengths and interests – much as many community colleges offering guided pathway programs do – to figure out who they are.

Guided pathways consequently appear to be a much better fit for students in this Job compared to those in the Help Me Get Away Job. It is uncertain, however, if colleges are properly customizing the pathway for students who already have clarity versus those who do not. These questions around whether guided pathways make sense – based on what Job a student has and based on the degree of customization for the student given her clarity within that Job – may help tease apart why guided pathway programs appear to be getting stronger results *on average* than traditional community college academic programs, but also why the data suggest that these structures do not work for everyone.[13]

The aspects of Wayfinding Academy's program that help a student discover who they are and where they go from here may be useful as well, but they may have to occur more quickly. A program that serves students with this Job must launch them into a clear pathway that allows them to step it up so they can do better and get away from a job, role, or habit now.

Entrepreneurs have a significant opportunity in this Job to build programs where traditional colleges and universities will not or cannot go because of regulations, standards, and legacy processes and priorities. The opportunity is at the "low-end" of the market where these programs are short, targeted, and focused and appear undesirable to traditional institutions.

The rise of coding bootcamps present a classic case study, as they use teachers who typically do not have doctoral degrees and could not become faculty members at many traditional institutions. These professionals are perfect for this Job because they are current in their industry knowledge, skills, and connections, given that they typically work in the tech industry and are therefore relevant to helping students step it up. There are enormous opportunities to create on-demand programs that help people at the moment they are stuck when they are most ready to learn with modular courses that can be customized based on where an individual student is going and based on what she already knows and can do.

The one place where entrepreneurs will likely struggle is in offering programs in fields where formal credentials are important. Established traditional institutions will have an advantage in navigating the regulations and bureaucracy.

HELP ME EXTEND MYSELF

On the surface, students in the Help Me Extend Myself Job are those that faculty members at institutions say they want to be teaching. The students in this Job are all about the learning – learning more and challenging themselves, pursuing a clear, concrete vision, and chasing specific, practical skills. They are here for the "right reasons," and they care intrinsically. This stands in stark contrast to many students in the Help Me Get into My Best School Job who may be far more interested in the extracurricular activities at the school, for example, or even the students in the Help Me Step It Up Job who are typically learning for extrinsic reasons.

At the same time, students in this Job often have a low commitment to what they are doing next. If the program does not work out or they do not learn what they want, it is typically no big deal. They are satisfied and can just go back to what they were doing. They are looking for low-risk programs as a result. All of this has important implications for the design of a program.

Institutions should focus on reducing anxiety so that their program is low-risk from a student's perspective. Features like a freemium model, a shopping week, or a three-week free trial like the one Purdue Global University has created,[14] in which students can try a program with no commitment to pay and see what the program will be like first, could help. Similarly, scholarships that reduce anxiety and make it easy to enroll could help as well.

Many of the students we spoke to also needed permission to enroll when they had this Job. Actively giving permission and reducing the anxiety of enrolling is important. Bay Path University, which has run a degree-completion program for women since 1999, has found that many mothers feel guilty about taking time away from their families to do academic work. Amanda Gould, Bay Path University's chief administrative officer, told the *Chronicle of Higher Education* that the "'No. 1 competition we have isn't other schools,' but prospective students' own doubts about whether they deserve to go to college.... 'We almost have to give them permission.'" Don't *almost* give them permission. Remember Sybil from Chapter 7 and give them unambiguous permission. Help prospective students alleviate self-conscious feelings about enrolling or tackle head-on questions that their family members or community may have about their decision to enroll.[15]

In many cases in this Job, earning a credential will be less important than the learning itself. This depends on the particular domain, but it is a good rule of thumb. Enrolling students and engaging them with material that connects clearly to their personal motivation will matter.

One piece of advice, therefore, is to make every class personal. This Job is about individuals bettering themselves. It is all about them, so make that emotional connection in both the course and in your marketing to students. Karen, the nurse we met in Chapter 6, loved her program because the projects she was doing helped her create a lasting legacy at her hospital. There was a direct connection. Bob had the same experience when he enrolled in the Stanford d.school. He is proud of the projects he did, which were related directly to the clients he was serving. The projects also helped him build confidence. As he said, "I didn't think I could do half of them" when he started. The satisfaction from having done them is immense.

Other ways to make the experience personal and engaging might be to make sure everyone receives a personal note from the professor. Make sure people can learn in small groups or in one-on-one sessions. Let students know that they are valued as individuals and that you are paying attention to them. People of course hire massive open online courses (MOOCs) and books to do this Job as well, but if the focus is on helping students complete, then personal touches should pay dividends.

The flip side of this is that because this Job is so personal, making it social might not be so important. By way of analogy, someone is not hiring a book club when she is in this Job. She is just hiring the book. Study groups or lots of whole-group interactions may not be desirable and might detract for students with this Job.

Similarly, because the commitment in this Job is low, be careful making things too hard. If you make something too hard, students will opt out. Following from these insights, high-stakes tests are likely not a good idea here, but short, frequent quizzes that are low stakes can be great. They show the students they are making progress and give them rapid feedback to build their understanding and solidify what they are learning. Capstone projects can be terrific, as well. Connecting those capstone projects to the individual's reason for enrolling is even better. The larger point is to not make this a miserable, externally driven exercise. And because students are not doing this for a grade in most cases, make sure you close the loop to ensure they are satisfied. That could be as simple as setting expectations up front about what they will accomplish. Then follow up with them at the end of a class or the program to have them recall what they were expecting and show them what they are now able to do after having completed the program.

Entrepreneurs have a huge opportunity to serve students with this Job. Many students will be looking for short, on-demand niche experiences that allow them to better themselves. Institutions have historically competed in this arena by offering everything from executive education programs, continuing education programs, and online courses to alumni cruises to far-away destinations with a professor (predominantly for retirees who likely experience this Job a lot) and static materials like books. Platforms that offer short learning experiences with capstone projects, frequent start dates, personal interaction, and a variety of topics might have significant potential to make in-roads.

The recent emergence of micro-learning, mobile-first experiences like Duolingo and the MBA from Smartly[16] could be perfect here. Platforms that offer personal teachers on-demand could also have a future. For example, Wyzant, an online site that matches tutors to students, has found that a number of its students hire the platform to do the following Jobs that relate to the Help Me Extend Myself Job: "Help me learn new skills so that I will be able to take on a new job in the future" and "Help me advance in my hobby or passion." With today's technology, it is possible for everyone to have their own personal teacher for any given subject at an affordable price, not just the wealthy and elite who can afford it or compel someone to offer it to them. You can have your go-to person for computers; your go-to person for a sport, music, or art; and your go-to people for extending yourself in your career. And you can have a personalized learning experience created just for you. Institutions that are stuck in time-bound traditions of semesters, credit hours, and fixed courses that have specific scopes and sequences as opposed to modular sequences that adapt to a student's own knowledge and skills will struggle to create these sorts of experiences.

WHY MOST COLLEGES MUST FOCUS

Colleges today are taking a lot of flak for their costs. One major reason for the escalating costs in traditional universities is the rise in administrative costs, or overhead. From 1987 to 2011–2012, nonacademic administrative and professional employees at universities more than doubled and far outpaced the growth in students or faculty. In New England, administrative salaries and wages grew more than twice as fast as student enrollment between 2007 and 2016 at private colleges. Spending like this is not only increasing the price of college, it is also increasing the cost at a time when institutions' business models are at a breaking point, as revenues cannot keep pace; the cost of educating a student is rising faster than family income and other sources of support.[17]

The rise in overhead is a function of many things – students who need more support, the cost of keeping up with the changes other peer institutions make, student expectations, and so on. **At a fundamental level, though, in any organization, high overhead costs result from managing significant complexity.**[18] Colleges and universities have become very complex places. Many aspire to become excellent in every field of research and instruction and to provide any course of study that any student might want. Managing, and actively supporting, students through the numerous pathways that they might take between admission and graduation is extraordinarily complicated. The beginning of a permanent solution for many colleges and universities is that they must choose in what areas they will be excellent – the essence of strategy. It is only through focus that institutions can reduce complexity and thereby substantially reduce costs.

Only a very small number of institutions will be able to compete effectively in the broad-spectrum research game against the likes of Harvard, Stanford, and MIT. Others will need to focus on fields where they can excel – whether that be in research or in teaching and learning.[19] Understanding the Jobs for which students hire an institution and focusing by Job gives institutions the ability to zero in on what matters to their key constituents. Schools that focus based on Job will likely find that many of the costly administrative supports they have bolted on to their core operations in recent years may be unnecessary – or may become part of their core operations, not overhead – because the root cause of their institutions' high costs is that they are not integrated properly to help students make progress.

As a result, many of the administrative functions they have added have been akin to treating symptoms of students' struggles, not the causal reason for them. Once institutions focus on a Job and structure themselves to address the causal reasons students are hiring their institution – and accordingly change everything about their operations, much as SNHU did – they may find that they can offer a better service at lower cost that results in far more students succeeding.

To this point, in many ways the focus on *cost* misses the larger point that postsecondary institutions are

not delivering enough *value* to students by helping them make the progress they desire in their particular circumstances. As Sandy Baum, a fellow in the Education Policy Program at the Urban Institute, a nonprofit think tank, said, "This is not really about college affordability.... The issue is that many people are starting college programs that they don't finish. And that's a terrible problem. So if all you know is, 'I'm supposed to go to college,' and you have no idea what you want to do and you go to a school that doesn't serve you well or you wander around and you take a bunch of classes and you end up with nothing, that's really not a good plan."[20]

As Austin Louis, one of Wayfinding Academy's first students, said, he dropped out of Babson College outside of Boston his second year because he "didn't feel like he was learning anything.... A lot of the reasons of why I have done things in the past has been trying to please my parents.... It's [instead] about who we are and why we do the things we do. What gets me most frustrated is seeing people that I care about, friends back home, that feel trapped in this dull, uninspired life."[21]

With an understanding of why students are choosing college, postsecondary programs have the opportunity to change that and help all students make the progress they are seeking toward a purposeful and fulfilling life. We are sure that we have not provided "the answer" for a specific institution in the pages of this book. But it is our hope that this book and chapter give institutions and entrepreneurs ways to see new opportunities to create more value for students and society.

Part IV

Conclusion

Chapter 11

Parting Advice for Learners and Educators

Struggling moments are the seeds of innovation.

Identifying Jobs is fundamentally about discovering people's struggles to make progress in their lives. Once we have surfaced a Job, then we can innovate to craft better solutions to help people make progress.

RECOMMENDATIONS, NOT BLUEPRINTS

The process of innovation is inherently uncertain. It is also a process, not an event. It involves continually designing, building, and experimenting to test critical assumptions and unknowns. It then involves reflecting, learning, and improving. As a result, this book does not present "the answer" or a foolproof, step-by-step blueprint for any given student in a particular Job or for an institution grappling to provide more value. We offer insights to help guide, but not direct definitively. As students and institutions innovate together, we will all learn more, and solutions for each of the Jobs will improve. As solutions improve and more options abound, specific advice – and even the Jobs themselves – will change continuously.

We have four overriding recommendations for students and postsecondary organizations, however, as we reach the end of this book on helping people make better decisions about their learning journey and helping institutions improve the value they offer students.

FOR STUDENTS

1. **A gap year might really help you.** By a gap year, we do not mean simply traveling to Europe or doing nothing. We mean a year of experiences to learn about yourself – what you like and do not like, what are your strengths, what is your purpose, and what pathways are possible. Partake in active experiences, such as bootcamps, internships and externships, apprenticeships, paid work, experiential learning opportunities, short courses, or community service. Eliminate what you do not want and reflect to figure out what you do. As this book has suggested, a gap year of this sort can be just what students who are trying to get away or do what's expected of them need to make progress. Recall Naomi's story. After enrolling in college to help her get away from home

and then dropping out, she essentially took an extended gap year. She started by working in Taco Bell and then moved from a veterinary clinic to a chiropractor clinic as a receptionist. Next, she worked with doctors and medical assistants in health-care offices before landing at a hospital. As she earned money, each of these stops taught her something about what she did and did not want, which then led her to enroll at a local university to earn a bachelor's degree and become a nurse.

Organizations are increasingly popping up that offer formal gap-year experiences, including Global Citizen Year, and Winterline. You can learn more at Gap Year Association. Colleges and universities are increasingly supporting the practice. Or you can take a page from Malia Obama, the daughter of President Barack Obama, and piece together your own gap year.

At the end of the year, if college is the right next step for you, it will still be there. Many students we talked to said that they went to college because it felt like the next logical step. They were on the train, and they just didn't know whether they should get off at the station. The reality is that the train runs regular routes. Life is a long journey, and as you branch out into the real world, the artificial rat race we have constructed around accolades and "being successful" becomes less relevant. The "train" that we have been led to believe we must stay on – and ride in the front car, no less – will still be waiting for us.

2. **It's worth embracing routes that take you off the "beaten path."** There is a reason "The Road Not

Taken" by Robert Frost is such a popular poem. Its advice is timeless.

> Two roads diverged in a wood, and I –
>
> I took the one less traveled by,
>
> And that has made all the difference.

As the stories in this book illustrate, life is not linear. There is no one path that makes sense for all. Broaden your options for what you could hire when you move into any of these Jobs. Far too many students, particularly those who were experiencing the Help Me Get Away, Help Me Get into My Best School, and Help Me Do What's Expected of Me Jobs, saw school as the only option.

Doing what everyone else is doing and limiting yourself to one option – standardization – flies in the face of what we know: you create unique value when you differentiate, and because we all have different learning needs at different times, are in different circumstances, and have different motivations, we need personalized pathways to help us all build our passions and fulfill our human potential. Have the courage to shirk what everyone else is doing to do what is interesting to you and valuable.

As you strive to broaden your options, focus on investing in yourself and learning, creating value, building productive relationships, and surrounding yourself with mentors to help you navigate your path. We have both been entrepreneurs, and we both would not be where we are today without the mentors we have had in our lives. If Bob could do it all over again, he would force himself to be an entrepreneur first, surround himself with mentors and advisors, learn what he did not know, and only then go to college. Michael would not be where he is today if he did not jump at certain career opportunities that had no clear pathway from them, but allowed him to be mentored by great people while doing valuable work about which he was passionate. Many of the people we profiled in this book who succeeded had an important person in their life support them – either a family member or an outside mentor – even if their path was not straightforward. An important takeaway is that we are all works in progress, and we never stop growing up. Don't artificially limit your opportunities. And remember that learning does not just happen in school. Family (your parents, children, siblings, and more), mentors, friends, colleagues, strangers, work, and life have plenty of lessons to offer. And if you choose work instead of school, you are also creating value, as measured by the fact that employers and customers are willing to pay for it. Holding a paid job means creating wealth and happiness for yourself and others. And you will be learning during it. Even if today's formal education system does not know how to recognize and value that learning, the education organizations of the future will increasingly.

3. **You are a lifelong learner.** You are not going to be in any one of these Jobs your whole life, but odds are that you will experience all these Jobs at some point in your life. That has perhaps always been true, but it is even truer today as the shelf life of skills

shrinks and the durability of degrees declines in the face of rapid discoveries; technological advancements like automation, artificial intelligence, and machine learning; and job changes that remake our economy. Put higher expectations on yourself *and* the entities through which you learn to meet you where you are today and where you want to go tomorrow. Do not settle. Demand the value you want. Value is the outcome one desires – in this case meaning the knowledge, skills, relationships, credentials, and so forth – divided by the resources spent attaining it – meaning time, money, energy, and the like. To make education better, we all need to be better consumers. When education is not good, one reason why is that we are not choosing in accordance with the progress we desire in our particular circumstance. In other words, we are not demanding good value. It is time to change the equation. Understand which Job you are experiencing and choose wisely.

FOR SCHOOLS AND LEARNING PROGRAMS, BOTH ESTABLISHED AND YET TO BE CREATED

1. **Acknowledge nonconsumption.** That is, recognize the number of people who need more education to make progress, but for whom a traditional college or university experience with a degree at the end is not the right way forward so they are not enrolling in colleges or universities today. Doing so means seeing that even as traditional colleges and universities in the United States bemoan the lack of public funding or

the coming demographic cliff where there will be far fewer "traditional" college students,[1] there are huge opportunities to serve more people more education. The stories and Jobs in this book give evidence to this.

To serve people in these Jobs, traditional schools will have to question many traditional processes, priorities, and structures that are often held sacred. But a deity did not deliver these traditions to civilization. They have not always been a part of human history. Some are relatively recent innovations. They were themselves created as solutions to a particular problem in a specific circumstance. When the problem or circumstance is different, the process or priority must be different as well. Being bound to tradition just because it has "always been done that way and has served us well" may not make sense. Colleges are wondrous places, so remaining true to the spirit of why a tradition was created may be wise. But being open to change the specific practice, priority, or organizational structure will be important to serve these nonconsumption opportunities. Given the increased need for lifelong learning and to skill up continually throughout one's career, the opportunities to serve nonconsumption will only multiply in the years ahead.

Many faculty and administrators at traditional colleges and universities today also bemoan that business leaders do not appreciate the value that they provide to students. According to one poll, a whopping 96% of academic officers believe their college prepares graduates for employment after school, whereas

11% of business leaders believe that recent college graduates are prepared for the workforce.[2] But this mismatch and criticism represent an opportunity for education institutions to see that as a struggle and their own opportunity to step it up, raise their standards, and innovate. The education organizations that lift the standards for employers – meaning what employers should expect from graduates – or find ways to de-risk the hiring decision for employers and reduce the friction in the system will have a big leg up.

2. **Change the admissions process and the orientation of how you serve students.** Enable people to acknowledge where they actually are in life and what they are trying to do. Do not make students grandstand in an effort to gain acceptance with statements of their capabilities and vision that fly in the face of where they really are. You can enable this by having each education program you offer focus on serving students in a particular Job – and then serving only students in that Job. If you are in a position to help students once you understand their actual circumstance and the progress they are seeking, then help them make that progress. If they are in a different Job from the one your program serves, then direct them elsewhere.

   Know your focus and strengths, and be honest about them and your limitations. Those limitations, stated positively, will help you reach the students you are best suited to serve, which is likely a much larger market than you serve currently.

It may be that you accept students who do not know what they want next, for example. Allow them to be honest about that. If you are the right school to help them figure it out, then do not let those students graduate until they figure out what is next. Support them in that process, but do not remove entirely the struggling moment for them by giving them "the answer." Remember, struggling moments are the seeds of innovation – for everyone. Individuals need to innovate in their own lives. Whatever you do, don't just take money from students to bounce around from major to major or wander aimlessly. That may bring in revenue in the short run, but it will destroy value in the long run. Today there is little downside for a school if a student takes a bad class, but there should be downside for a school that does not live up to its promise of helping students.

3. **As you reorient, raise your standards for students.** This may seem counterintuitive given the last piece of advice around honesty in the admissions process. It is in fact entirely consistent with it.

What we mean is that schools should set clear standards for graduating and hold to them. We don't mean only around academics, either. Students are not just functional beings, but emotional and social ones as well. If your program is designed to help people discover whom they are and what they want to do next, do not let them graduate until they have done that. Be true to who you say you are and accordingly support your learners.

And be rigorous. Make sure people truly master what it is they do at your school – be it an academic topic, a life skill, or understanding oneself. Learning is hard, and it is humbling. Yet somehow we have confused the time spent at an institution or teaching – both inputs – for learning, which is an outcome. We often act as though just because a teacher has appeared in front of students and lectured or because students were enrolled somewhere for four years that the students were ready to learn and have learned. Because of how our education system has unfolded over the past 150 years, many if not most students have not been prepared to learn for a long time now. As the institution serving them, it is time to take responsibility to make sure the student is ready to learn and will learn and then appropriately serve her. That is the opposite of the sorting function many schools today fulfill in which they sort students out from certain majors, for example, when a professor decrees that they do not have the right stuff and fails them. It is also the opposite of the phenomenon of when schools inflate grades.

A story from our friend Steve Spear, a senior lecturer at MIT, which appears in his book Chasing the Rabbit, helps illustrate what we mean. While a doctoral student, Steve took temporary jobs working first on an assembly line at one of the Detroit Big Three automaker plants and then at Toyota at the passenger-side front-seat installation point.[3]

In Detroit, the worker doing the training essentially told Steve, "The cars come down this line every 58 seconds, so that's how long you have to install this seat. Now I'm going to show you how to do it. First, you do this. Then do that, then click this in here just like this, then tighten this, then do that," and so on, until the seat was completely installed. "Do you get how to do it, Steve?"

Given he had a master's degree in mechanical engineering from MIT, Steve thought he could do each of those things in the allotted time. When the next car arrived, he picked up the seat and did each of the preparatory steps. But when he tried to install it in the car, it would not fit. For the entire 58 seconds he tried to complete the installation but couldn't. His trainer stopped the assembly line to fix the problem. He again showed Steve how to do it. When the next car arrived, Steve tried again but didn't get it right. In an entire hour, he installed only four seats correctly.

One reason why it was historically so important to test every product when it came off the end of a production line like the Detroit Big Three's was that there were typically hundreds of steps involved in making a product, and the company could not be sure that each step had been done correctly. In business, we call that end-of-the-line activity "inspection." In education, we call it "summative assessment."

When Steve went to work at the same station in Toyota's plant, he had a completely different experience. First, he went to a training station where he was told, "These are the seven steps required to install this seat successfully. You don't have the privilege of learning step 2 until you've demonstrated mastery of step 1. If you master step 1 in a minute, you can begin learning step 2 a minute from now. If step 1 takes you an hour, then you can learn step 2 in an hour. And if it takes you a day, then you can learn step 2 tomorrow. It makes no sense for us to teach you subsequent steps if you can't do the prior ones correctly."

Assessment was still vital, but it was an integral part of the process of learning. As a result, when he took his spot on Toyota's production line, Steve was able to do his part right the first time and every time. Toyota had built into its process a mechanism to verify immediately that each step had been done correctly so that no time or money would be wasted fixing a defective product. It therefore did not have to test its products when they came to the end of the production process.

That is quite a contrast between the two methods for training Steve Spear. At the Detroit Big Three plant, the time was fixed, but the result of training was variable and unpredictable. The "exam" – installing the seat – came at the end of Steve's training.

At Toyota, the training time was variable. But assessment was interdependently woven into the learning, and the result was fixed; every person who went through the training could predictably do what he had been taught to do.

The Detroit example represents how most of America's schools operate. They were modeled on factories built during the Industrial Revolution. The Toyota example illustrates more how a competency-based, or mastery, learning system would work. Many postsecondary programs should move to a system in which students progress when they have mastered whatever the objective is. This may not matter today for many students in the Help Me Get into My Best School Job who are often enrolling for the experience, not the learning, of college, or for a segment of those in the Help Me Extend Myself Job where whatever they learn is gravy, but for most students in most Jobs, this would be helpful. And the central message can carry over to whatever a school claims it does for students' growth, even if much of that value lies outside of the traditional academic classroom.

Schools must recognize that learning will not always be linear, and there will be a variety of reasons students may struggle at times. Support them in filling in gaps in their knowledge and skills with personalized pathways that adapt to their needs. That could be through adaptive learning software – a functional solution – or tutoring platforms like Wyzant that provide tutors that do not just help with remediating knowledge and skills for students but also provide strong relationships that help students work through their struggles. It also means recognizing that students will need help in figuring out who they are and what they want next – and that the lack of knowing may be the cause of failure more than any knowledge gap. Creating structured gap years, particularly those that offer financial aid or even pay and offer credit, could be a critical part of supporting students in this journey. But regardless, career and life planning must become a part of students' educational journey. Today, traditional colleges and universities do virtually no career planning at all. The average career services office has an annual operating budget of just $90 000 with only one counselor for every 2917 students.[4] Little wonder only half of students ever visit the career services office at their campus.[5]

Instead, good schools will make students do their career and life planning on the way in – and then make sure the planning is interwoven with the curriculum throughout. That means that students should understand what they are really signing up for when they declare a major – for example, what it will really mean to be an accountant – before they have gone through most of the courses and realize they hate it but they are stuck with it because of all the debt they have incurred. To tackle the lack of satisfaction that students have with their undergraduate education that we discussed in Chapter 2, schools should move upstream to guide students in their journeys far earlier – not just at the end of their schooling. By moving upstream, schools can understand the root cause for students' dissatisfaction, which typically doesn't show up until much later. With that understanding, the schools can then guide the students to success, as opposed to being focused on preventing failure. There is a large and growing industry in higher education around preventing failure. But we do not eliminate risk by focusing on risk. We eliminate it by understanding causality and tackling that. Dumbing down standards is not the answer.

There is another important part of the Toyota story. Each step in the production of a Toyota car has an obligation to reject any vehicle where a prior step was completed wrongly and send it back to that prior station on the assembly line where it's fixed. Colleges and universities should begin to do the same and push high schools and other feeder schools – be those community colleges or undergraduate programs – to raise the rigor bar and move to a mastery-based system. Within colleges, individual classes and professors should force prerequisite classes to do the same. Ultimately, this would have a powerful influence by raising standards across the system and creating embedded rework stations at every step of the educational process – not remedial classes where students who do not pass certain tests are sent to take non-credit-bearing classes, which often dooms them to fail in college.

FORGING AN EDUCATIONAL MARRIAGE

As the saying goes, "In politics, as in love, timing is everything." The same is true in education.

Education is ultimately a two-sided process. That is similar to when someone is trying to find a spouse. The progress someone is seeking must overlap with the progress a potential partner is seeking. There is a matchmaking process on both ends where a given education program may be outstanding at something, but for it to be the right program for you, it has to be the right fit at that time and circumstance in your life. Similarly, a student may be outstanding in many facets, but if she is not the right fit for what your school does, then it is not a match.

A debate has raged in education circles for years about whether "college for all" – such that we do not lower expectations for students from low-income or minority backgrounds – makes sense, or if that movement is flawed because it moves everyone into the same slot, even though the college slot is not a good fit for every student, and career or technical training might be a better next step.

Both sides of the debate have some merit, but the Help Me Do What's Expected of Me and Help Me Get Away Jobs overwhelmingly show that college cannot be a destination unto itself just because it is what you are supposed to do. Too many students enter into situations that are not right for them, and they do not fundamentally buy the narrative. Committing to a four-year school and taking on lots of debt for something about which you lack passion is unwise. It is irresponsible to continue peddling the narrative that everyone should go to college instead of focusing more deeply on helping students build passion and purpose and explore alternative pathways to success – while avoiding the soft bigotry of low expectations.

This does not mean that college will never be the right step for someone. College and, more to the point, education can help bring a lifetime of happiness. But that education has to be the right focus at the right time and in the right circumstance for both parties. An individual's struggles are not something to be ignored, but to be harnessed to allow all of us – individuals, schools, and society – to innovate and make progress. Creating false dichotomies serves no one.

Far better is for individuals to know where they are in their lives, what they want, and how to articulate it, and for an education program to state clearly when and how it can and cannot help you. Neither side today is speaking the right language. Schools must understand what students are really trying to do, and students must understand what schools can provide. If we can facilitate the conversation in society – between the lifelong learner, families, employers, and universities – then we can help improve education everywhere.

Only then can we ensure that education delivers on its promise of helping people build their passions, fulfill their human potential, and live a lifetime of productive struggle and happiness.

Appendix: How to Unearth a Job

The choice to get more education – or where to get that education – is, as we've illustrated, complicated.

The five Jobs we discovered in our research process are assuredly not the only Jobs for which people hire higher education. And, as we have stated, each Job has texture, nuance, and variation within it. A deep dive on the Jobs students hired one particular college to do would likely yield subsegments of some of the Jobs. But this list of five Jobs – what is driving people to get more education – emerged clearly and distinctly over many months of research and analysis.

In this appendix, we offer more detail about the Jobs to Be Done theory – both from a theoretical and practical perspective as well as a behind-the-scenes look at our research process for those who are interested.

THE FORCES AND TIMELINE THAT COMPRISE A JOB TO BE DONE

Jobs to Be Done aren't things that you can discover by hypothesizing about them in the abstract. Life is messy.

What pushes and pulls people toward new solutions and the habits and anxieties that hold them back are too complicated to divine in a theoretical or abstract way. Until you do the research with real people making a real decision, you just won't know what the Jobs really are.

To identify Jobs, you have to look at the actual moment – and all the events that led up to and after that moment – someone decides to take action and make a switch from her current solution or behavior to a new one. That allows us to "see" a Job as it occurs in someone's life.

As we decide to "hire" a new solution and "fire" an old one, there are four forces acting on us, as depicted in Figure A.1. We discussed these forces throughout the book, but the graphic helps visualize how these forces interact with each other.

As we wrote in Chapter 5, there are two forces moving us toward a new solution, *compelling change*:

1. **The push of the situation.** This is the struggling moment that causes us to want to make a change. The push of the situation involves things *right now* in our life that are causing us to be dissatisfied. That dissatisfaction is significant enough that it drives us

Figure A.1 Forces compelling and opposing change.

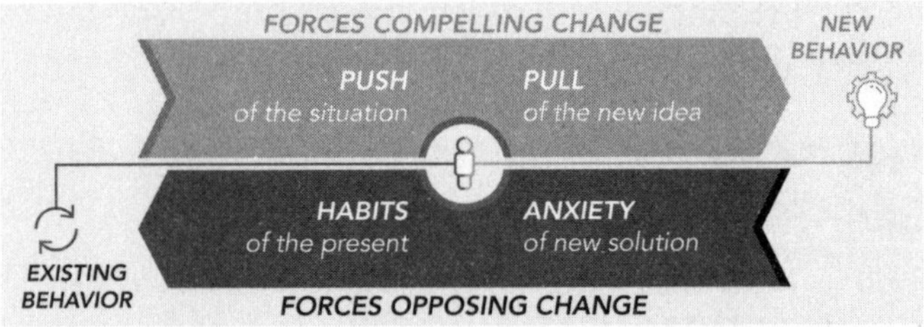

to change something in our life so that we can make progress in a different way.

2. **The pull of a new solution.** This is the allure of something new. It's what causes us to see something we can jump to when our current situation is not working for us. Without the pull of something new, we just stay on a treadmill thinking that we have to do something different, but not acting. The new solution has to be relatively enticing. It must create enough magnetism so that we can see how it can improve our lives. Even in Jobs where people are largely pushed to make a change as opposed to pulled – think of the Help Me Get Away Job, for example – a pull still exists. In the Help Me Get Away Job, the presence of college as a potential solution creates that pull even though the student may not have visited the school or know what she would do once there. Recall how in Chapter 5 Naomi glamorized the beauty of a school she had never visited. What's important to understand is that the push in the Help Me Get Away Job – I have to get away from something in my life – is so strong that the pull required to spur action and choose a college is relatively low. But there is still some pull.

Organizations typically spend a lot of time focusing on the pull of a situation. They add more features to try and entice people to the new solution.

But just as, if not more, important in causing a switch is addressing the last two forces, those *opposing change.*

3. **The anxiety of the new solution.** As we think about a new solution, we start thinking inevitably about all the

things that we might not be able to accomplish with it. Will the new solution deliver on its promises? Will we be able to use it? Is it too expensive? How will we learn to use something so new? The anxiety – that fear of the unknown – creates friction around adopting anything new. All too often organizations forget to reduce anxiety or even ask us about our fears around something new. As we wrote, anxiety could play a large role in creating paralysis when someone experiences the Help Me Extend Myself Job. Eliminating features of a product or service can actually often reduce anxiety because they might be overwhelming. "There's just too much stuff!" you might say. Some health clubs, for example, have realized recently that locking customers into annual contracts creates so much anxiety that it prevents them from joining in the first place.

4. **The habit of the present.** "I'm used to doing it this way," or "I don't love this, but at least I know it works," are classic habits of the present. The thought of switching to a new solution is almost too overwhelming. Sticking with the devil we know, even if imperfect, is bearable. In the case of the Help Me Extend Myself Job, sticking with the devil we know is more than bearable – it's a perfectly acceptable option, which is why it's important to overcome someone's anxiety with a frictionless solution.

The other key framework to understand is the Jobs to Be Done timeline. Almost every decision we make to consume something new occurs through a set of phases, as depicted in Figure A.2.

Figure A.2 Jobs to Be Done timeline.

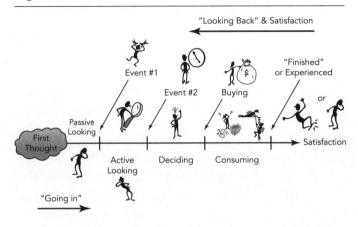

First Thought: We have a first thought that it's time to make a change. That thought might stem from realizing that high school is ending soon, seeing older friends go to school, or starting to understand that our current job isn't allowing us to afford the lifestyle on which people around us are depending.

Passive Looking: After the first thought, we enter a phase of passive looking. We are thinking about doing something new or buying something to help us make progress. We will definitely look at buying a new solution if it comes along, but we are not actively pursuing it.

Event 1: Next, some sort of event occurs – for example, you have to sign up for the SAT, or your friend and fellow colleague at work gets laid off. The event triggers a response: it's time to act and do something about the situation.

Active Looking: This then triggers a phase of active looking where we invest time and energy into figuring out what to do about the struggle we are having and the progress we would like to make. Many people who sign up for a free massive open online course (MOOC) but don't watch anything past the first video, let alone complete, are likely actively looking – or what we might call shopping. They have not yet made the decision to hire a new solution to help them make progress.

Event 2: Another event occurs typically that introduces a time-based element to your decision, as it creates criteria around what will happen and when. For example, if you are a senior in high school who has been accepted to a couple of colleges, seeing your best friend commit to a college might define the time horizon at play for you to make a decision in a visceral, concrete way.

Deciding: The second event sends us into a phase of actually making a decision.

Buying: We then buy. We commit firmly and pay for the new solution.

Consuming: After buying, we (ideally) consume the new solution. That's when we can assess how satisfied we are with the decision we made and learn if a college or other educational program was the right fit.

HOW TO "WATCH" WHAT PEOPLE DO AND "SEE" THE JOB TO BE DONE

Although it would be great to watch people in real time as they work through the Jobs to Be Done timeline and hire a solution – as Bob was able to do with those who hired milkshakes – it's often hard to watch what people do.

So how to overcome the fact that what people say they want is unreliable at best?

Interview to Create a Timeline of the Decision-Making Process

We interview people, but instead of asking them what they want in a particular service, we create a story – or mini-documentary – of their education-buying process so that we can "see" what they did. That allows us to see their *actual* priorities through the tradeoffs they make and thus what they actually valued, not what they might *say* was important.

Most of the students we interviewed had recently enrolled in school, so their selection process was fresh in their minds. This helped us capture an accurate rendering of their struggle to choose and the timeline of the events – as depicted in Figure A.2 – that led to their decision.

In the interviews, we never said simply, "Tell us about your college and why you chose it," or something like that. We instead had the students tell us the story of how they chose as though they were living through the decision again. By doing this, a student could not say "Oh, the drama program really appealed to me," even though that wasn't something she considered when she made her decision.

We instead used the interviews to look for the dominos in people's decisions. What were the events that tipped in a causal way to bring the student to where she was now? Oftentimes people will say something mattered to them, like cost, but when you look at the moment of purchasing an experience, they opt for a more expensive option. It's worth repeating. *What is important is to watch what people do, not what they say.* That means deploying various techniques, like those from criminal forensic interviews, to learn what really happened. We also unpack the ambiguous words people use to describe certain experiences so that we can understand what people really mean. For example, if someone says he went to a campus because it was "cool," what does "cool" mean? Can he provide examples of what is not cool? The impact of these sorts of questions is to force people to build language around what they would say are intuitive things that drove them to their decision. We are making ambiguous phrases concrete.

IDENTIFY THE ENERGY IN SOMEONE'S DECISION

A goal of the interview is to identify the *energy* in a person's decision to see what *causes* them to move along the Jobs timeline from a first thought that something could be better, to looking, and then finally to deciding and switching behavior. As we summarize in Chapter 4, energy is equal to the effort someone expends in making a decision times the magnitude of that decision divided by the time horizon over which it was made (Figure A.3).

Not everything that is a significant factor in someone's life, for example, relates to the Job at hand. Something that happened in the past may be significant in a person's *life*, but she is unable to explain why she chose to do something different *now*. To understand why someone made their decision when they did, we dug beneath surface-level explanations for why people chose college to discover the causal mechanisms that drove them. We looked at

Figure A.3 Energy invested in making a decision.

Energy = Effort × Magnitude of Decision/Timeline of Decision

both a student's desired future, but also their current circumstance, as energy can emanate from both. For example, if a time horizon in which to make a decision gets compressed, that can create energy, which can cause someone to take an action she might not have if the time horizon had been more stretched out. Maddy, whose story we tell in Chapter 4, chose to go to a college about which she was not excited because her friends had all committed to going to school in the fall, for example. She did not want to be the only one still at home. Spotting this social energy and the corresponding time frame allowed us to understand the progress she was seeking to make in her situation.

Maddy's example illustrates why it is so important to dig for the energy that causes the switch in the functional, emotional, and social elements that drive behavior. The art of the interview is in trying to capture and make sense of that movement. What are the buckets of energy that led someone to desire something, be fearful of something, need to get away from something, and so forth? It is critical to keep an eye on the energy that relates to the circumstance at the moment of choice.

It is also important to understand the sets of energy together in each story. There is almost never just one thing that causes someone to do something. People make decisions for multifaceted reasons. Just because your parents went to a school or because all your friends are going there does not, by itself, dictate where you will go.

WHO WE INTERVIEWED

In our research, we initially interviewed 108 students. These students had a range of biographical backgrounds that mirrors the diversity and vastness of American postsecondary education today.

They attended everything (see Figure A.4) from community colleges (23%) to public and private four-year colleges (50%) and from online programs (12%) to bootcamps (5%) and historically black colleges and universities (10%).

Not unlike many students nationwide, many of the 108 students had attended multiple colleges and postsecondary education experiences in their lives. We formally captured and coded 209 of those different stories, which provided 103 different educational institutions in our sample.

Although demographics do not determine destiny or one's circumstance and Job – people experience many of these Jobs at different times throughout their lives – we

Figure A.4 Interviewees by type of institution. (Because some of these categories overlap, numbers do not add up to 100%.)

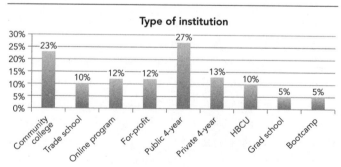

used demographics to our advantage to be sure we caught a wide array of different situations in which people pursued postsecondary education.

Similar to the demographics nationwide that attend college, our initial sample of 209 stories (see Figure A.5) contained more female stories than male – 64% female and 36% male, compared to 57% and 43% nationwide.

Just over half – 54% – of our sample (see Figure A.6) were white, 22% were black, 16% Hispanic, and 14% were Asian. That compares to the national numbers of 55% white, 14% black, 16% Hispanic, and 6% Asian.[1] Eight percent of our sample were immigrants, 12% were the children of immigrants, and 4% spoke English as a second language.

Figure A.5 Interviewees by gender.

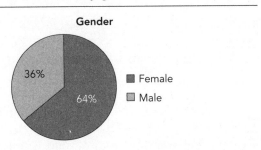

Figure A.6 Interviewees by race. (5.3% of the stories in our sample were of people of mixed race.)

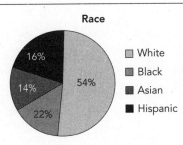

Figure A.7   Interviewees by age.

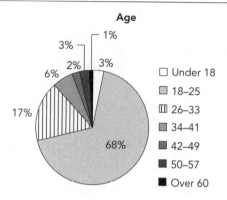

Just over 70% of the stories in our sample were of people under the age of 25 (see Figure A.7) – 10 percentage points higher than the national average. Seventeen percent were 26–33, with the remainder over 34.

We formally interviewed one student who was over 60. Eighteen percent had at least one child, which tracks with the finding that roughly a quarter of undergraduate students have at least one child, according to the Institute for Women's Policy Research.[2]

Sixty percent of the sample was of students who were lower-middle class, working class, or poor. Seventy percent lived off campus, and, similar to national numbers, 33% attended part-time. Fifty-five percent worked a part-time job, multiple part-time jobs, or a full-time job while they attended. Forty-six percent were first-generation college students, which means their parents did not complete a bachelor's degree.

The vast majority of participants (see Figure A.8) in our research – 92% – had a high school diploma; a few people had earned a GED. Thirty-four percent had some college

Figure A.8 Interviewees by education.

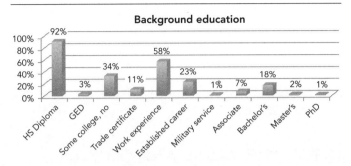

Background education

but no degree, and 58% had prior work experience. In line with the increasing reality that postsecondary education doesn't necessarily mean college, 7% had an associate degree, 18% already had a Bachelor's, 2% had a Master's, and 1% had a PhD.

The students we interviewed and stories we heard, in other words, went far beyond the ones we typically read about in the mainstream media or see in Hollywood movies from *Animal House* to *Old School* of grassy-green quads filled with 18-year old students who live in dorms and attend school full-time. That helped us gain a broad view of why students pursue postsecondary education.

HOW WE CHOSE THE STUDENTS WE INTERVIEWED

We reached the 108 students by partnering with nine different institutions – eight postsecondary education programs and one company that serves students attending hundreds of institutions around the country and world. At each institution, we deployed a screening survey to identify and select students for the interview who had a lot of energy around the college decision-making choice – what design thinking[3] would call the "extreme users" – so that we would be able to observe users with a real struggle around attending postsecondary education such that we would not miss key motivations that might go unnoticed in people who had less energy or struggle around their decision.

INTERVIEW, CODE, AND CLUSTER

Each interview lasted roughly an hour, and we paid the participants for their time. We focused on the energy that moved the timeline forward and coded each interview for the pushes and pulls that were present. We also paid close attention to what habits and anxieties were holding them back. As we coded the forces of progress, we used their language, not ours. Overall, we identified nearly 40 different forces of progress, which we list on the last page of the appendix. The pushes are represented by "When I … " statements, as they refer to a struggle or tension in one's current circumstance, and the pulls are represented by "So I can … " statements, as they refer to what a solution would allow someone to do.

From there, clear patterns emerged. We were able to create clusters of like interviews where there was high overlap of the forces of progress present or absent – in other words, the stories in each cluster shared a pattern of causality that led the students to make the decisions they did. Five clusters emerged, which were the five Jobs we identified. We then dove into each of those clusters to understand how they were alike and different from each other and walked through all of the stories that fell into each cluster so we could gain a greater understanding of the dimensions of the different Jobs. In the book, we list out the top five pushes and pulls for each Job.

We also layered the demographics back into the Jobs, not to predict a student's motivations, but to develop different personas – semifictional representations of a "typical" student – within each Job that would give us more depth into understanding a Job's context.[4] This helped us offer advice for students experiencing these different Jobs, as well as give advice to institutions of how to design solutions that would get the Job done.

Finally, we checked ourselves by conducting more interviews. We talked to roughly 30 more students to see if their stories would fit into the Jobs that had been identified. Different researchers conducted some of these interviews. Then we collected even more data by deploying quantitative surveys in which well over 1500 students responded. We kept the data from this subsequent research separate from that in our initial research.

In the book, we give each student a fake name so as to preserve anonymity. With the exception of the University of Texas, where we were given explicit permission to name the school, we avoid giving the name of the schools the students attended, as well as other important details, to protect their identity. The other reason we have done this is so that as you read the stories, you didn't get so swept up in the details of any one student's story that you could not see yourself and a situation that you may have experienced or are experiencing in them. We want you to be able to identify with the core elements that make each Job different from one another so that when you are contemplating choosing more education, you can figure out which Job you are in and make a wiser decision.

The Forces of Progress Identified

1. When I need to take the next logical step

2. When I don't have/can't see any other options

3. When I got experience/exposure and thought, "I'd be good at that"

4. When I need to get out of this job/role/habit

5. When I'm doing well in my job/career/business, but I want a better one

6. When I am directed by a trusted advisor

7. When I have time and can fit it into my life/schedule/budget

8. When I don't have confidence

9. When I'm afraid of where things are headed (sick of living paycheck to paycheck)

10. When it's so easy/cheap/obvious, I can't see why not

11. When this isn't me/I need to step it up/I know I can do better

12. When I am ready now/at last

13. When I need to satisfy/obey people in my life

14. When I have earned/deserve this opportunity

15. When time is running out/it's now or never

16. When I need to get away (from this home/town/family/relationship)

17. When it's time to grow up and be an adult

18. When I need a break from the daily grind

19. When I feel increasing pressure to be responsible and that people depend on me financially

20. So I can check the box

21. So I can learn more/challenge myself

22. So I can get specific, practical skills/certifications

23. So I can pursue a clear, concrete vision

24. So I can better understand a subject/field

25. So I have a safety net/something to fall back on

26. So I can make people in my life proud

27. So I can find my passion/purpose

28. So I can belong to a place with prestige/a great reputation

29. So I can build my confidence

30. So I can reinvent myself and meet new people

31. So I can enroll in a great program in my discipline

32. So I can live in a brick-and-mortar college

33. So I can be with people like me

34. So I can have the support I need

35. So I can have the classic "college experience"

36. So I can build my network

37. So I can enjoy the athletics/travel/extracurriculars

38. So I can live in a location and maybe stay there

Acknowledgments

This book would not have been possible without the tireless work of Audrey Hall, a former research assistant at the Clayton Christensen Institute, a nonprofit think tank. Audrey conducted interviews, analyzed and coded data, contributed to our thinking, and remained an email away to help us clarify any questions we had as we worked to finalize the manuscript.

The support of the Christensen Institute more generally was critical to this project happening. The Institute provided funding, as well as vital research support and helpful colleagues. Michelle Weise, formerly a senior research fellow at the Institute, was the early visionary behind this project and helped shape the research design and secure funding. Julia Freeland Fisher, a researcher at the Institute, was an important thought partner as we developed the ideas, and she provided valuable input on the manuscript. Cliff Maxwell, Clay Christensen's chief of staff, also provided critical input on the manuscript. Our colleagues Alana Dunagan, Richard Price, Lisa Hicks, Ann Christensen, Hayden Hill, Tom Arnett, Chelsea Waite, Jenny White, and Meris Stansbury all played important roles in furthering this book and its impact.

The Christensen Institute is a special place where researchers use theories of innovation to tackle an array of the challenges confronting society. We're grateful for all of our colleagues and their work, as well as the space the Institute provides to do important projects like this book.

We both owe a huge debt of gratitude to Harvard Business School Professor Clayton Christensen himself. Clay has been a mentor to both of us in our lives and brought us together over a decade ago. He developed the Jobs to Be Done theory that forms the core for the insights in this book with Bob Moesta in the mid-1990s at Harvard and brought Michael Horn into the field of education when they coauthored *Disrupting Class* and together founded the Clayton Christensen Institute. Clay is a voice and model of wisdom, humility, and kindness. His theories help guide our lives on a daily basis. We are also grateful to him for writing the Foreword for this book.

In addition, we are also thankful for the team that, along with Clay, wrote *Competing Against Luck,* which explains the Jobs to Be Done theory. We offer a special thanks to Karen Dillon, who provided critical feedback on the manuscript.

We owe our gratitude to the ReWired Group as well, which Bob founded and where he is the CEO. On a daily basis the ReWired Group helps clients around the world create value in the lives of consumers, and the team there spent valuable time helping us develop the ideas and insights in this book. Ervin Fowlkes spent countless hours up-front helping develop the interview protocol and research design. Greg Engle and Matt Sheppard pushed the analysis forward in important ways.

We also extend our thanks to The Entangled Group, an education venture studio, where Michael is the head of strategy. Paul Freedman, Gunnar Counselman, Nick Hammerschlag, Mike Berlin, Mat Frenz, Lauren Dibble, Lauren Pizer, Jasmin Schiener, Kara Foley, Allison Salisbury, and Terah Crews helped advance the ideas in this book, conduct further Jobs to Be Done interviews, and prototype early surveys that informed the development of the tool we have provided to help you figure out which Job you are experiencing right now. Jeff Selingo, Michael's partner on the podcast "Future U," provided invaluable advice.

We had a number of other readers of the manuscript who provided important insights and edits. Larry Horn spent many hours not only reviewing the initial draft manuscript but also subsequent versions to help us get the tone right. Tracy Kim Horn, Jonathan Haber, and Helen Kemp provided important feedback and edits on the manuscript as well.

Thank you also to the team at Wiley. Our editor, Pete Gaughan, offered important support in shaping the manuscript. And Amy Fandrei was tireless in helping us get everything just right – from the cover design to the title and marketing plan. We thank Anne Hoffman (Dean of the Relay Graduate School of Education in San Antonio) and Krista Williams (school psychologist for Liverpool Central Schools in Fayetteville, New York) who gave valuable insight that strengthened the manuscript as peer reviewers.

We thank Tejal Mistry for creating the illustrations in the book.

Kristen Karp and Danny Stern, our literary agents at Stern Strategy Group, were once again critical partners in the process of bringing this book to fruition. They care deeply about the work they do and the ideas and people they support, which make them wonderful friends and supporters. Ned Ward, Dan Masi, Whitney Jennings, Rachel Auerbach, Brian Hyland, Brian Sherry, Alison Amyx, Stephanie Heckman, and many more at Stern Strategy Group provided support as well to help promote the important messages from the book to improve the lives of learners and their families, as well as colleges, universities, and all learning organizations. Thanks to Alan Lowenthal as well for his advice throughout the process.

We also thank Jason Palmer, a general partner at New Markets Venture Partners, who took a chance on this project when he was the deputy director in the Postsecondary Success strategy at the Bill & Melinda Gates Foundation. We appreciate the foundation's support of the early research behind this book.

Finally, a big thank you to all of the institutions – colleges, universities, bootcamps, and education service providers – that allowed us to interview their students. Although we cannot name some of the institutions, we thank the University of Texas-Austin and Harrison Keller, deputy to the president for strategy and policy; Southern New Hampshire University and its president Paul Leblanc; Western Governors University and its president Scott Pulsipher; the University of West Georgia; and General Assembly for their support.

Michael B. Horn and Bob Moesta

Thank you to my friend, and now coauthor, Bob Moesta. When Bob and I met in a diner in Watertown over a decade ago for breakfast, I could tell immediately he was a special person. I had no idea how much he would change my life and how I see the world. He's become not only a friend, but also a mentor and source of wisdom and creativity. I'm glad we did this book together, and I'm thankful for the many opportunities we have to collaborate.

Thank you to my mom and dad for their continued support, modeling, and inspiration. My father, Larry Horn, dug in to help us refine this book on top of his already busy work schedule, and I'm very appreciative that he went beyond anything anyone should ever expect. It brought me back to moments in elementary, middle, and high school when he helped teach me to write. He's a tough editor, and there's no one better. He's always been my role model in life, and I'm glad to have benefited from his generosity, critical eye, and love.

My wife, Tracy Kim Horn, continues to be an inspiration and thought partner in my work. She always tells it to me straight and never hesitates to dig in on reading what I've written – and tell me how I could make it better. Listening to her is one of life's joys and benefits. I love you, and thank you.

Our daughters, Madison and Kayla, are the joys that light up our lives and give extra meaning to my work. When it comes time for them to choose college, I will be thrilled at whatever path they choose to take so long as they choose in accordance with the progress they, and they alone, are seeking to make. I hope my contributions toward making education more student-centered, such that all learners can build their passions and fulfill their human potential, benefit them. Madison and Kayla, I love you.

I would be remiss if I didn't thank Susan Kim, Joonki Kim, Megan Lynch, and Tova Weinronk who helped provide support to our family so that I could finish this book.

Finally, I dedicate this book to the memory of my late grandparents, Grammy and Papa. Along with my parents, they afforded me the opportunity to have choices in my education that were meaningful and beneficial and set me on my course in life. There isn't a week that goes by when I don't think of and miss them. Their memories are a source of strength and joy, a blessing and a comfort.

Michael B. Horn
Lexington, Massachusetts

This book marks a shift in how I'm focusing my time and energy. For the last 30 years, I've helped companies build products for consumers. But over the last couple of years, I realized that if I was to look at my bucket list, a big item was to help consumers become better consumers. This book is the first of more work to come around helping people understand *why* they are doing *what* they are doing so that they can make better choices to make progress, and we can be a better society with less waste in the world. Education, health care, housing, and careers are all things we need to get better at choosing, and I'm intent on helping.

This is a book for today's context as people try to figure out what to do next in their lives – should they go back to school and where should they go? The world and surrounding context will almost certainly change, but my hope is that this is the beginning of how education will transform, as we all become better consumers. It's time to enable students to take control of their education so that we can all be and do better.

I dedicate this book to my mother, who was the ultimate of all teachers. I am dyslexic. My mother recognized this and knew the consequences of being labeled in the 1970s with a learning disability. She taught me how to learn creatively in my own ways and hack the education system to make progress and get through it.

I've learned that dyslexia is in some ways like cancer. It's a broad label that describes many different types of learning disorders that impact the ability to read. We are all learning disabled in our own way. Although today's education system was designed to focus on the masses, the tails are where innovation happens. I am passionate about enabling all of us to think in our own way.

I thank my third grade teacher, Ms. Lopiccolo, who knew I was different and enabled me to take my own path to figure things out.

I also thank Anita Gildea, formerly of Houghton Mifflin Harcourt. Roughly a decade ago, Anita brought me in to help with a project in grades 9–12. As a dyslexic who struggled my way through both K–12 and higher education, I felt I had no place to help in education because I had been such an outcast while there as a student. Anita showed me that I could make a positive impact in the world of education.

I thank my wife for her tireless support, guidance, and lifelong partnership. I know I'm exhausting, and I appreciate that your energy is more than mine.

Thank you to my kids for helping me through the act of getting all four of you into college, which was another foundational piece of this book, as I realized how many different perspectives there are around college, how many choices exist, and how hard it is to choose.

My team at the ReWired Group is an amazing bunch. I thank them for constantly helping me think through, reframe, and improve the thoughts in my head. Thanks to Rick Pedi, John Beaumont Palmer, Julia Wesson, Pam Murtaugh, and Marg Treloar, who were all there in the beginning, as well as to Chris Spiek and Greg Engle. A special thanks as well to Ryan Singer at Basecamp for being an on-demand thought partner.

I also thank Jon Palmer, Clay Christensen's former chief of staff, and Harvard Business School Professor Derek Van Beaver, who is the director of the Forum for Growth and Innovation, a research project that Clay Christensen guides. They have offered me countless support, not just for this project, but for many of the projects I have had at the Harvard Business School. Their fingerprints are on much that I have done.

I also owe a special thanks to Dr. W. Edwards Deming and Dr. Genichi Taguchi for taking me in as a 19-year old, mentoring me for years, and believing in me to enable me to think, learn, and be who I am today.

Finally, thank you to Michael Horn for many things, but first for being able to take the thoughts and analysis in these topics and put words to them. Though I can speak to these ideas, Michael has written them very eloquently. Michael brings a brilliant and practical navigation of the education space, and we make a great team of the mad professor and the artful navigator.

Bob Moesta
Grosse Pointe, Michigan

About the Authors

Michael Horn speaks and writes about the future of education and works with a portfolio of education organizations to improve the life of each and every student. He serves as the head of strategy for the Entangled Group, an education venture studio, and as a senior partner for Entangled Solutions, a strategy consultancy for the education ecosystem. He is also the co-founder of and a distinguished fellow at the Clayton Christensen Institute for Disruptive Innovation, a nonprofit think tank.

Michael is the author and coauthor of multiple books, white papers, and articles on education, including the award-winning book *Disrupting Class: How Disruptive Innovation Will Change the Way the World Learns* and the Amazon-best-seller *Blended: Using Disruptive Innovation to Improve Schools*. An expert on disruptive innovation, online learning, blended learning, competency-based learning, and how to transform the education system into a student-centered one, he serves on the board and advisory boards of a range of education organizations, including the Clayton Christensen Institute, the Robin Hood Learning + Tech Fund, and the LearnLaunch Institute.

He also serves as an executive editor at Education Next and is a venture partner at NextGen Venture Partners.

Michael was selected as a 2014 Eisenhower Fellow to study innovation in education in Vietnam and Korea, and *Tech & Learning* magazine named him to its list of the 100 most important people in the creation and advancement of the use of technology in education. Michael holds a BA in history from Yale University and an MBA from the Harvard Business School.

Bob Moesta is an innovator, entrepreneur, and the co-creator of the Jobs to Be Done Theory to investigate consumers' motivations and decision-making processes. The co-founder and president of the ReWired Group, Moesta helps leaders and companies repeatedly innovate and reliably predict and drive lasting success.

An experienced product developer and engineer by training, Bob has worked on and helped launch more than 3,500 new products, services, and businesses across nearly every industry, including education, health care, defense, auto manufacturing, software, financial services, and construction.

Bob is a guest lecturer at The Harvard Business School, MIT Sloan School of Entrepreneurship, and Northwestern University's Kellogg School of Management. He holds degrees from Michigan State University and the Harvard Business School. He has studied extensively at Boston University's School of Management, MIT School of Engineering, and Stanford University's d.school. He and his wife, Julie, have four children and live outside Detroit.

Notes

CHAPTER 1

1. As our friend Paul Freedman, cofounder of the Entangled Group, discovered in his research, often people's final destination for an education is constrained by their initial top pick – meaning that if you have your heart set on New York University (NYU), even if you do not go to NYU or one of its peer institutions, you are likely to find yourself in college in a major city that is or resembles the Big Apple.

2. We recommend the recent book by our colleagues Julia Freeland Fisher and Daniel Fisher, *Who You Know: Unlocking Innovations That Expand Students' Networks*, San Francisco: Jossey Bass, 2018, as well as Michael Horn and Heather Staker, *Blended: Using Disruptive Innovation to Improve Schools*, San Francisco: Jossey Bass, 2014, to start you thinking about school redesign. *Who You Know*, in particular, paints a picture of the need to expand intentionally students' social capital and view of potential life opportunities by weaving that in the design of schools.

CHAPTER 2

1. The industry around helping students pick college was not around a couple generations ago. As Frank Bruni recounts, there were not shelves of books to help people choose college back in the 1960s. "Against the backdrop of the current obsession with college admissions, it's funny to be reminded how little thought many spectacularly successful people put into where they went to school." Frank Bruni, *Where You Go Is Not Who You'll Be: An Antidote to the College Admissions Mania*, New York: Grand Central Publishing, 2016, pp. 81–83.

2. Jeffrey J. Selingo, 2017, *There Is Life After College: What Parents and Students Should Know About Navigating School to Prepare for the Jobs of Tomorrow*, New York: HarperCollins, Kindle Location 597.

3. "*69.7 percent of 2016 high school graduates enrolled in college in October 2016*," Bureau of Labor Statistics, https://www.bls.gov/opub/ted/2017/69-point-7-percent-of-2016-high-school-graduates-enrolled-in-college-in-october-2016.htm, May 22, 2017.

4. "Table 187: College enrollment rates of high school graduates, by sex: 1960 to 1998," https://nces.ed.gov/programs/digest/d99/d99t187.asp.

5. According to Forbes, the SAT prep industry was valued between $1 billion and $4 billion in 2014, Caroline Howard, "Right answer for SAT? College board revamps test, partners with Khan Academy," *Forbes*, March 5, 2014, https://www.forbes.com/

sites/carolinehoward/2014/03/05/right-answer-for-sat-college-board-revamps-test-adds-partnership-with-khan-academy/#13355f215d5f.

6. National Association for College Admission Counseling, "College Applications", In 2017 State of College Admission, 2017, https://www.nacacnet.org/globalassets/documents/publications/research/soca17_ch1.pdf.

7. Ariel Kaminer, "Applications by the dozen, as anxious seniors hedge college bets," *New York Times*, November 15, 2014, https://www.nytimes.com/2014/11/16/nyregion/applications-by-the-dozen-as-anxious-students-hedge-college-bets.html. Also see Bruni, p. 52.

8. James Davi Vance, *Hillbilly Elegy: A Memoir and a Family and Culture in Crisis*, New York: Harper-Collins, 2016, pp. 154–155.

9. President Obama's Address to Joint Session of Congress, February 24, 2009, http://www.washingtonpost.com/wp-srv/politics/documents/obama_address_022409.html.

10. Selingo, Kindle Location 381. Anthony P. Carnevale, Stephen J. Rose, and Ban Cheah, *The College Payoff: Education, Occupations, Lifetime Earnings*, The Georgetown University Center on Education and the Workforce, https://cew.georgetown.edu/wp-content/uploads/2014/11/collegepayoff-summary.pdf. Anthony P. Carnevale, Ban Cheah, and Andrew R. Hanson, *The Economic Value of College Majors*,

Georgetown University Center on Education and the Workforce, 2015, https://cew.georgetown.edu/wp-content/uploads/Economic-Value-of-College-Majors-Full-Report-v2.compressed.pdf.

11. Beth Akers and Matthew M. Chingos, *Game of Loans: The Rhetoric and Reality of Student Debt*, Princeton, NJ: Princeton University Press, 2016, Kindle Location 897. Jaison R. Abel and Richard Deitz, "Despite Rising Costs, College Is Still a Good Investment," Liberty Street Economics, June 5, 2019, https://libertystreeteconomics.newyorkfed.org/2019/06/despite-rising-costs-college-is-still-a-good-investment.html?cid=db

12. Akers and Chingos, Kindle Location 919.

13. Selingo, Kindle Location 1102.

14. "5 Things You Need to Know About College Admission," The College Board, https://bigfuture.collegeboard.org/get-in/applying-101/5-things-you-need-to-know-about-college-admission.

15. Bruni, p. 54.

16. Akers and Chingos, Kindle Location 447.

17. Goldie Blumenstyk, *American Higher Education in Crisis?: What Everyone Needs to Know*, New York: Oxford University Press, 2015, Kindle Location 738.

18. Tamara Hiler and Lanae Erickson, "What free won't fix; Too many colleges are dropout factories," Third Way, August 11, 2016, http://www.thirdway.org/report/what-free-wont-fix-too-many-public-colleges-are-dropout-factories.

19. Emily Hanford, n.d. "Some college, no degree," American RadioWorks, http://americanradioworks .publicradio.org/features/tomorrows-college/ dropouts.

20. Blumenstyk, Kindle Location 361–364.

21. "From 1987 to 2010, sticker price tuition and fees ballooned from $6630 to $14 510 in 2010 dollars. After subtracting institutional aid, net tuition and fees still grew by 92%, from $5720 to $11 000. To provide perspective, had net tuition risen at the rate of much maligned health-care costs, tuition would have only risen 32% to $7550 in 2010." Grey Gordon and Aaron Hedlund, "Accounting for the rise in college tuition," National Bureau of Economic Research, November 13, 2017, http:// www.nber.org/chapters/c13711.pdf, p. 2. Also, "net tuition for full-time students increased eight straight years at public four-year institutions, seven straight for students at public two-year colleges and for six straight years. Also, "net prices for full-time students at public four-year institutions have increased for eight straight years, for seven straight years for students at public two-year colleges, and for six straight years for those at private nonprofit colleges and universities. So the typical student keeps paying more for college each year." Rick Seltzer, "Net price keeps creeping up," *Inside Higher Ed*, October 25, 2017, https://www.insidehighered.com/news/ 2017/10/25/tuition-and-fees-still-rising-faster-aid- college-board-report-shows.

22. Blumenstyk, Kindle Location 654.

23. Deirdre Fernandes, "College-bound? The fees could end up being a big surprise," *Boston Globe*, August 20, 2018, https://www.bostonglobe.com/metro/2018/08/19/college-bound-the-fees-could-end-being-big-surprise/aOzer5MwbAyhNyWlwIc3UO/story.html.

24. Akers, Kindle Location 919.

25. Akers, Kindle Locations 447, 826.

26. Ryan Craig argues in *A New U: Faster + Cheaper Alternatives to College*, Dallas: BenBella Books, 2018 that the college premium has reached its peak and is now declining. Goldman Sachs suggested in a research note in 2015, for example, that students in 2010 could expect to recoup their college investment in eight years, but the trend has been negative and grown to nine years. And the annual Census data shows that the average earnings differential between high school and four-year graduates rose sharply until 2000 to $32 900, but then fell to $29 687 by 2015.

27. Selingo, Kindle Location, 193.

28. Burning Glass Technologies and Strada Institute for the Future of Work, "The Permanent Detour: Underemployment's Long-Term Effects on the Careers of College Grads," 2018.

29. Blumenstyk, Kindle Location 332–334.

30. Courtney Connley, "Google, Apple and 13 other companies that no longer require employees to have a college degree," CNBC, August 16, 2018, https://www.cnbc.com/2018/08/16/15-companies-that-no-longer-require-employees-to-have-a-college-degree.html.

31. Education Consumer Pulse, *On Second Thought: U.S. Adults Reflect on Their Education Decisions*, Strada Education Network and Gallup, 2017.

32. NCES Fast Facts, "Back to school statistics," http://nces.ed.gov/fastfacts/display.asp?id=372, Many students – nearly 40% of undergraduates – also attend part-time, as they work or balance family responsibilities as parents. Blumenstyk, Kindle Location 449–455.

33. Wendy Erisman and Patricia Steele, "Adult College Completion in the 21st Century: What We Know and What We Don't," Higher Ed Insight, June 2015, p. 2.

CHAPTER 3

1. Jennifer Medina, Katie Benner, and Kate Taylor, "Actresses, business leaders and other wealthy parents charged in U.S. college entry fraud," *New York Times,* March 12, 2019, https://www.nytimes.com/2019/03/12/us/college-admissions-cheating-scandal.html.

2. Frank Bruni, *Where You Go Is Not Who You'll Be*, New York: Hachette, 2016, p. 174.

3. Bruni, p. 192.

4. As blogger John Warner, wrote, "When college was primarily the province of the privileged, the preparation was college itself, a kind of finishing school for the gentry, majors be damned." John Warner, "Before we end majors as we know them," Inside Higher

Ed, May 23, 2018, http://insidehighered.com/blogs/
just-visiting/we-end-majors-we-know-them.

5. Jeffrey J. Selingo, 2017, *There Is Life after College: What Parents and Students Should Know about Navigating School to Prepare for the Jobs of Tomorrow*, New York: HarperCollins, p. 160.

6. Bruni, pp. 14–41, 162.

7. Bruni, p. 241.

8. Kyle Spencer, "It takes a suburb: A town struggles to ease student stress," *New York Times*, April 5, 2017, https://www.nytimes.com/2017/04/05/education/edlife/overachievers-student-stress-in-high-school-.html.

9. See also Donna St. George, "Longtime leader of 'overachievers' stepping down at Walt Whitman High," *Washington Post*, June 17, 2018, https://www.washingtonpost.com/local/education/longtime-leader-of-overachievers-stepping-down-at-walt-whitman-high/2018/06/17/160c16e4-6fca-11e8-bd50-b80389a4e569_story.html?utm_term=.54c76650ff41.

10. Richard N. Bolles, *What Color Is Your Parachute? 2019*, New York: Ten Speed Press, 2018, p. 47.

11. A 'Fit' over rankings: why college engagement matters more than selectivity, Challenge Success, Stanford Graduate School of Education, October 2018.

12. Bruni, p. 93.

13. Bruni, pp. 100–101.

14. Bruni, pp. 183, 193.

15. Bruni, p. 192.

CHAPTER 4

1. Yoni Cohen, "5 reasons keeping a gratitude journal will change your life," *Happify Daily* (https://www.happify.com/hd/why-you-should-write-a-gratitude-journal, accessed March 11, 2019).

2. Sara Lamback, Carol Gerwin, Dan Restuccia, *When Is a Job Just a Job – And When Can It Launch a Career: The Real Economic Opportunities of Middle-Skill Work*, Jobs for the Future, Lumina Foundation, Burning Glass Technologies, June 2018 (https://jfforg-prod-prime.s3.amazonaws.com/media/documents/Resume DataBook6.pdf).

3. Our friends at IDEO who started The Purpose Project, a course for high school students, told us this story. See https://thepurposeproject.org.

4. Julia Freeland Fisher and Daniel Fisher, *Who You Know: Unlocking Innovations That Expand Students' Networks*, San Francisco: Jossey Bass, 2018.

5. Tom Vander Ark, "The world of work – In elementary school," *Forbes*, October 17, 2018, https://www.forbes.com/sites/tomvanderark/2018/10/17/the-world-of-work-in-elementary-school/#75bc3842d128.

CHAPTER 5

1. Bill Burnett and Dave Evans, *Designing Your Life: How to Build a Well-Lived, Joyful Life*, New York: Knopf, 2016, Chapter 6.

CHAPTER 6

1. James David Vance, *Hillbilly Elegy: A Memoir and a Family and Culture in Crisis*, New York: Harper-Collins, 2016, Kindle Locations 2106, 2136.

2. We give credit to Bill Burnett and Dave Evans for phrasing this insight just right in *Designing Your Life: How to Build a Well-Lived, Joyful Life*, New York: Knopf, 2016.

3. As star tennis player Serena Williams said, "Everyone draws their passion in different ways. It's important to pay attention to things that make you happy." Katherine Schwarzenegger, *I Just Graduated ... Now What? Honest Answers from Those Who Have Been There*, New York: Crown Archetype, 2014, p. 213.

4. Burnett and Evans, Chapter 3.

5. Research by J.W. Pennebaker from the University of Texas and Stephanie Spera, a psychologist with an outplacement firm, helped to show the power of this approach. Duncan Mathison and Martha I. Finney, *Unlock the Hidden Job Market: 6 Steps to a Successful Job Search When Times Are Tough*, Upper Saddle River, NJ: Pearson Education, 2010, pp. 44–47.

6. Richard N. Bolles, *What Color Is Your Parachute? 2019*, New York: Ten Speed Press, 2018, pp. 44, 48.

7. Tom Rath, *StrengthsFinder 2.0*, New York: Gallup, 2013, p. 2.

8. Kevin W. McCarthy, *The On-Purpose Person: Making Your Life Make Sense*, Winter Park, FL: On Purpose Publishing, 2013, pp. 57, 73.

9. Burnett and Evans, Chapter 2.

10. Brooke Howell, "Finding your purpose at work: An interview with Imperative CEO Aaron Hurst," https://www.monster.com/career-advice/article/imperative-ceo-aaron-hurst-0825. We also recommend checking out the resources that Project Wayfinder, built in partnership with the Stanford d.school to help people discover their purpose. Visit https://www.projectwayfinder.com.

11. Bolles, pp. 85–87.

12. Viktor Frankl, *Man's Search for Meaning*, Boston: Beacon Press, 2006, p. 98.

13. Burnett and Evans, p. 118. All of Chapter 4 is useful for this step.

14. Bolles, pp. 121–122.

15. As Bolles wrote in *What Color Is Your Parachute?*, "[Careers] that sound terrific in your imagination don't always look so great when you actually see them up close and personal." p. 125.

16. Adele Faber and Elaine Mazlish, *How to Talk So Kids Will Listen & Listen So Kids Will Talk*, New York: Scribner, 2012, p. 139.

CHAPTER 9

1. Clayton M. Christensen, Taddy Hall, Karen Dillon, and David S. Duncan, *Competing Against Luck: The Story of Innovation and Customer Choice*, New York: HarperCollins, 2016, Chapter 2.

2. Allison Aubrey, Class divide: Are more affluent kids opting out of school lunch? *NPR*, September 9, 2015, https://www.npr.org/sections/thesalt/2015/09/09/438578867/class-divide-are-more-affluent-kids-opting-out-of-school-lunch.

3. Clayton M. Christensen and Michael E. Raynor, *The Innovator's Solution: Creating and Sustaining Successful Growth*, Boston: Harvard Business Review Press, 2003, Kindle Location 1235–1249.

4. Christensen et al., *Competing Against Luck*, pp. 50–56, 156.

5. Christensen et al., p. 158.

CHAPTER 10

1. Wayfinding Academy, https://wayfindingacademy.org.

2. Jeffrey Young, "This new 2-year college is unlike any other. And that could be its biggest challenge," EdSurge, March 30, 2018, https://www.edsurge.com/news/2018-03-30-this-new-2-year-college-is-unlike-any-other-and-that-could-be-its-biggest-challenge.

3. Wayfinding Academy, "Complete college in 2 years with Wayfinding Academy!" https://www.goabroad .com/providers/wayfinding-academy/programs/ complete-college-in-2-years-with-wayfinding-academy"percnt;21-162119.

4. The number of nonacademic administrative and professional employees at universities more than doubled from 1987 until 2011–2012, far outpacing the growth in students or faculty. Jon Marcus, "New Analysis Shows Problematic Boom In Higher Ed Administrators," New England Center for Investigative Reporting, *Huffington Post*, February 6, 2014, https://www.huffingtonpost.com/2014/02/06/ higher-ed-administrators-growth_n_4738584.html.

5. David L. Clinefelter, and Carol B. Aslanian, "*Online college students 2017: Comprehensive data on demands and preferences,*" The Learning House, Inc., Louisville, KY, 2017, p. 26, OCS-2017-Report.pdf

6. See, for example, Laura Krantz, "Small colleges are struggling financially, and they can't raise tuition high enough to fix it," *Boston Globe*, August 11, 2018.

7. Nathan D. Grawe, *Demographics and the Demand for Higher Education*, Baltimore: Johns Hopkins Press, 2017.

8. Ethan Knight, the executive director of the Gap Year Association, suggests purpose occurs at the intersection of understanding what a student loves

to do, what they are good at, what they can be paid for, and what the world needs. Project Wayfinder has also developed tools and a course that colleges can use to help students discover their purpose. Visit www.projectwayfinder.com

9. Purpose Project, https://thepurposeproject.org.

10. Sydney Johnson, "More bootcamps are quietly coming to a university near you," August 2, 2017, https://www.edsurge.com/news/2017-08-02-more-bootcamps-are-quietly-coming-to-a-university-near-you.

11. Incidentally, there is a question of whether the metaphor of the "gap year" should be rethought, as Abby Falik, founder and CEO of Global Citizen Year notes. If we stop viewing education as a strictly linear path, then viewing the year experience isn't so much a "gap"—or a break from something—as it is the presence of a formative learning experience in people's lives that ideally stretches their boundaries through a blend of novel experiences, mentorship, and self-reflection.

12. The New School, a nonprofit research university in New York City, offers a gap year program for which it grants students credit. But the learning done in that program, in which students explore the language and culture of Costa Rica, is unlikely the fit for students in the "Help me get away" Job who need a clearer set of short experiences.

13. Goldie Blumenstyk, *The Adult Student: The Population Colleges—and the Nation—Can't Afford to Ignore*, The Chronicle of Higher Education, 2018, pp. 22–23.

14. See https://www.purdueglobal.edu/about/risk-free-trial.

15. Blumenstyk, *The Adult Student*, p. 20.

16. Michael Horn is an advisor to Smartly. Smartly might also be a great candidate for students in the "Help Me Step It Up" Job.

17. Seton Hall Professor Robert Kelchen, an expert in higher education finance and accountability, makes this point in an article in the Boston Globe. Laura Krantz, "At many small colleges, administrative spending is surging," *Boston Globe*, August 29, 2018, https://www.bostonglobe.com/metro/2018/08/28/administrative-spending-outpaces-student-enrollment-growth-across-new-england/ip1C7OT0 8ACGXH3o0EfBJO/story.html?et_rid=490881002& s_campaign=todaysheadlines:newsletter.

18. Clayton M. Christensen, Michael B. Horn, Louis Caldera, and Louis Soares, *Disrupting College: How Disruptive Innovation Can Deliver Quality and Affordability to Postsecondary Education*, Center for American Progress, February 2011.

19. Adapted from "Disrupting College," p. 52.

20. Sydney Johnson, "Beyond Tuition: How Innovations in College Affordability Are (or Aren't)

Helping Students," *EdSurge*, June 12, 2018, https://www.edsurge.com/news/2018-06-12-beyond-tuition-how-innovations-in-college-affordability-are-or-aren-t-helping-students?utm_source=EdSurgeInnovate&utm_medium=email&utm_campaign=06-13-18&mkt_tok=eyJpIjoiWmpNeE4ySXlNbUppTnpWbCIsInQiOiJKaENUYnk0QjhSM2ZveG0yd2JXbnRWXC9KUDFUVXkyUzRIcVBncVpvTHpqTFhqUlJNTXUxbkp3V0k0VG1ldGpxT0JNdGGxSaFRlZFwvYlVmUEJLV2QxMWtlUFk5UlR3c2hEbEddBXC9CNHJOU0pBbVwvVEdpTGJtR1UreEVoYWtU3aCtRUlUifQ%3D%3D.

21. Young, March 30, 2018.

CHAPTER 11

1. Nathan Grawe, *Demographics and the Demand for Higher Education*, Baltimore, MD: Johns Hopkins University Press, 2018.

2. Brandon Busteed, "Higher education's work preparation paradox," *Gallup-Lumina Foundation Poll on Higher Education*, February 25, 2014, https://news.gallup.com/opinion/gallup/173249/higher-education-work-preparation-paradox.aspx.

3. This story is adapted from Clayton M. Christensen, Michael B. Horn, and Curtis W. Johnson, *Disrupting Class: How Disruptive Innovation Will Change the Way the World Learns*, New York: McGraw-Hill, 2010, pp. 108–109.

4. Jeffrey J. Selingo, "Reimagining the career center: How colleges can better engage and prepare a new generation of students for the 21st century," Entangled Solutions, July 2017, p. 7.

5. Doug Lederman and Paul Fain, 'A new U: faster + cheaper alternatives to college': A Q&A with Ryan Craig, investor and author of a new book about the changing landscape for education and training credentials and the implications for traditional higher education, Inside Higher Ed, August 22, 2018, https://www.insidehighered.com/digital-learning/article/2018/08/22/qa-ryan-craig-author-new-book-faster-cheaper-college.

APPENDIX

1. "Table 306.10 total fall enrollment in degree-granting postsecondary institutions, by level of enrollment, sex, attendance status, and race/ethnicity of student: selected years, 1976 through 2014," *Digest of Education Statistics, National Center for Education Statistics*, https://nces.ed.gov/programs/digest/d15/tables/dt15_306.10.asp?current=yes.

2. Elizabeth Noll, PhD, Lindsey Reichlin, MA, and Barbara Gault, PhD, "College Students with Children: National and Regional Profiles," p. 1, https://iwpr.org/wp-content/uploads/2017/02/C451-5.pdf.

3. IDEO, the famous design firm, defines design thinking as a process for creative problem solving

by utilizing elements from a designer's toolkit like empathy and experimentation.

4. Although marketers often start by developing personas – a semifictional representation of the ideal customer based on market research about existing customers – the problem is that demographics don't *cause* people to consume services. It's better to start with the Job to Be Done – an understanding of what causes someone to consume – and then layer in personas underneath the Job to give more depth and context to the particulars so it's easier to see how best to serve different people who have the same Job.

Index

H

Habit, of present, 226, 228
Hall, Taddy, 179
Harvard Business School, 44, 153, 169
Harvard's Extension School, 159
Healthcare, 110–111, 113, 114, 194
Help, 5–8
Help Me Do What's Expected of Me Job, 60, 63; ambivalence in, 71; apathy in, 71; assumption in, 67–68; career variety and, 82; check and choose in, 78–79; choice or, 76–77; competency-based degree in, 69–70; delayed acceptance and, 66; design experiences for, 190–192; dissatisfaction in, 64, 73–74; dream school and, 64–66, 72, 84–85; entrepreneur educators and, 192; without excitement, 67; gap year or, 76–77, 82, 190–191; gratitude in, 64–65, 74–75; identify matches in, 76–78; know thyself in, 75–76; logical step in, 71–72; math major in, 185; motivation in, 70–71; options in, 68; parents in, 82–85; passion and, 78–81, 83, 85; pathways in, 78–81, 192; personas in, 72–73; pressure in, 64, 84; price in, 83, 191; safety net in, 72; self reinvention and, 67; time horizon in, 78, 83; transfer and, 67, 78–79, 191; visits in, 65–66; at

Wayfinding Academy, 183; working adults and, 77
Help Me Extend Myself Job, 6, 29, 135, 185; capstone projects in, 202; check and choose in, 146–147; clarity of, 140–141; colleagues in, 147–148; commitment of, 200, 202; design experiences for, 200–204; emotional connection in, 201; entrepreneur educators and, 203–204; Help Me Get into My Best School Job compared to, 200; Help Me Step It Up Job compared to, 141; identify matches in, 145–146; know thyself in, 145; learning for learning's sake in, 136, 201; math major in, 186; moms in, 144; negotiation in, 146–147; online programs and, 186; opportunities in, 136–138; paralysis in, 146; parents and, 147–150; permission in, 147–148, 150, 200–201; personal connection in, 201–204; pulls in, 142–143; pushes in, 142–143; risk of, 141–143, 146, 200; self challenges in, 140; success in, 144–147; Wyzant for, 203
Help Me Get Away Job, 6, 29, 80–81, 83, 240; bootcamps in, 194–195; check and choose in, 99–102; comfort of, 89; commitment in, 95–96, 99, 102–103; community colleges and, 97,